THE RELIGIOUS SPEECHES OF
BERNARD SHAW

✻✻✻✻✻✻✻✻✻✻✻

Bernard Shaw in 1907

THE
RELIGIOUS SPEECHES OF

BERNARD SHAW

Edited by Warren Sylvester Smith
Foreword by Arthur H. Nethercot

The Pennsylvania State University Press
University Park, Pennsylvania
1963

Library of Congress Catalog Card Number 63–18890

Copyright 1963 by the Public Trustee as Executor of the Estate of George Bernard Shaw. Published by The Pennsylvania State University Press by license of the Public Trustee. Composed and printed in the U.S.A.

Since I have heard Shaw speak I know that . . . [he] is not a rocket, as is believed in Germany. He is a holy fire watched over by a cold intelligence.

—Hermann Barr (1911)

❋❋❋❋

FERROVIUS: The Christian god is not yet. He will come when Mars and I are dust; but meanwhile I must serve the gods that are, not the God that will be. . . .

THE EMPEROR: Very wisely said. All really sensible men agree that the prudent course is to be neither bigoted in our attachment to the old nor rash and unpractical in keeping an open mind for the new, but to make the best of both dispensations.

THE CAPTAIN: What do you say, Lavinia? Will you too be prudent?

LAVINIA: No: I'll strive for the coming of the God who is not yet.

—*Androcles and the Lion* (Act II)

FOREWORD

✳✳✳✳

It is only within the last decade that devoted Shavian students in any numbers have followed the lead of James Fuchs, set in 1926 in his collection of fugitive speeches and articles entitled *The Socialism of Bernard Shaw,* and have produced similar collections of Shaw's less-known obiter dicta on music and musical critics, on theater, on Shakespeare, on "platform and pulpit," and even on Ireland. It is only natural and proper, therefore, that the present collection of his lectures on religion should offer valuable and welcome new material to the insatiable Shavians. It is probable, too, that this collection will do a great deal to correct the continuing misconception of much of the general public about Shaw as a rationalist, a skeptic, an unbeliever, an agnostic, and even an atheist. No intelligent person, after reading these speeches, could regard him, in his mature years, as anything but a genuinely religious man, even though his definition of religion was a pretty broad and unorthodox one. But *orthodox,* properly defined, as Shaw's orthodox friend G. K. Chesterton once pointed out, means "right thinking." Shaw was always certain that his thoughts on every subject were right, though his youthful views on religion later became modified to a much greater extent than those on most other subjects.

    Several years ago, in the course of a talk to the Shaw Society of London, I casually referred to Shaw as both a cynic and a mystic, and during the discussion period afterward I was indignantly challenged on both counts—by two different people. Somewhat to my surprise, as the argument developed, I discovered that the critic who was unwilling to accept him as a cynic was perfectly willing to accept him as a mystic and that the critic who was unwilling to accept him as a mystic was only

✳vii

too willing to accept him as a cynic. Eventually the rest of the audience agreed that he was both, just as, in *The Quintessence of Ibsenism,* after distinguishing carefully between the idealist and the realist, Shaw, citing Shelley as an example, pointed out that an individual might be an idealist in some matters and a realist in others.

After reading these lectures, especially "The Religion of the Future" of 1911, no one could doubt Shaw's mysticism, for in it he states dogmatically, "As for my own position, I am, and always have been, a mystic." The title of this lecture also settles another question often raised about Shaw: Did he regard creative evolution, with its attendant doctrine of the life-force, as a philosophy or a religion? Although in his *Sixteen Self Sketches,* in an article on his religious faith written while he was in his nineties, he refers to Bergson as "the established philosopher of my sect," there is no doubt that, as the very title, "The Religion of the Future," reveals, he regarded creative evolution as primarily a religion.

The phrasing of this title also suggests another interesting aspect of the present lectures: Many times certain ideas and even certain passages in them reappear in the plays and their prefaces. In the preface to *Back to Methuselah* in 1921, for instance, Shaw maintains that creative evolution is not merely the religion of the future but "the religion of the twentieth century." The idea of the heterogeneity of religions in the Empire, expressed in both "The Religion of the British Empire" in 1906 and "Modern Religion II" in 1919, is reworked into one of the most amusing passages in *The Simpleton of the Unexpected Isles* in 1934. The statement in "The Religion of the Future" that we "may regard the typhoid bacillus as one of the failures of the life-force that we call God, but that the same force is trying through our brains to discover some method of destroying that malign influence" is a refining and elevating of a similar statement about the croup in *The Shewing-Up of Blanco Posnet* in 1909. The disagreement of Newton and Hogarth over whether the "line of nature" is a straight line or a curve, as debated in "Religion and Science," Shaw's tribute to Einstein in 1930, is reworked in *"In Good King Charles's Golden Days"* in 1939, but transferred to Newton and Kneller (and Barbara Villiers) because, unfortunately for Shaw's chronological plan, Hogarth did not paint until the next century.

The alert reader of these previously uncollected talks on religion by Bernard Shaw will undoubtedly discover many other ideas which relate to the better-known Shaw of the plays and their prefaces and the polemical prose works.

ARTHUR H. NETHERCOT

Evanston, Illinois
May 9, 1963

ACKNOWLEDGMENTS

✴✴✴✴

The editor wishes to express gratitude to Mr. Dan Laurence and Mr. Stanley Weintraub for help and advice; to Mr. and Mrs. Archibald Henderson and to Mr. LaFayette Butler for the use of materials in their collections; to Mr. Bertram Hammond, present curator for the City Temple in London; and to the Council on Research of The Pennsylvania State University for financial support.

For permission to reprint the editor is indebted to the firms of C. A. Watts & Company, Ltd., and The Pioneer Press, London; to the *New York Times;* and especially to the Public Trustee and The Society of Authors on behalf of the Shaw Estate. A conscientious search was made to locate heirs to the copyrights of defunct periodicals, but without success.

CONTENTS

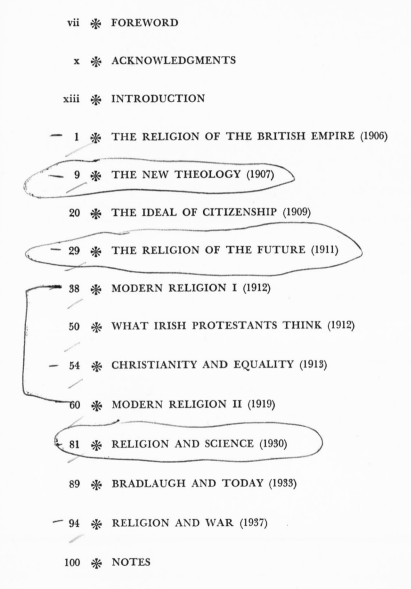

INTRODUCTION

****

When Bernard Shaw left Ireland in 1876 to join his mother and sister in London, he moved into the geographical center of a religious and intellectual turbulence almost without precedent. The great intellectual revolution of the time was of course world-wide, but London seemed to be its focus. Although the effect of the revolution on the religious attitudes of most Victorians has probably been overstated,[1] the effect on the people with whom Shaw associated in the last decades of the nineteenth century was profound.

Shaw himself had no religion when, at the age of 20, he arrived at Victoria Grove. Ten years later, addressing the Shelley Society, he still called himself an atheist. Yet he never joined the vigorous secularist movement, although he often supported its champions and their reforms, nor did he join any of the religiously oriented groups, even though he frequently sided with their leaders. Such behavior was not unusual. It was common for the Christian Socialist to denounce the secularist as the Antichrist on Sunday and come to his aid in establishing free evening classes at the London School Board meeting on Monday.

Reform-minded Victorians with a joining instinct had a wide choice of social and religious movements. Arthur H. Nethercot has cataloged most of them in his biography of Annie Besant,[2] but even she, with her intense desire for the better world, could not sample them all. The socially conscious and dissatisfied intellectual of the time could select in the secularist movement alone branches led at various times by G. W. Foote, George J. Holyoake, Charles Watts, and W. Stewart Ross, in addition to Charles Bradlaugh's National Secular Society, and could with good conscience also belong to the Ethical Society, the Fellowship of the New Life, or the Zetetical Society. He could advocate causes, with or without religious overtones, in the Humanitarian League, the Land Nationalization Society, the Land Reform Union, the Law and Liberty League, the Malthusian League, or the Society of the Friends of Russia and might also join the growing Cooperative Movement, though many socialists considered its program a makeshift substitute for reform. Even within socialism, the intellectual could choose the Social Democratic Federation (claiming to be the most truly Marxist), the Socialist Union or the Socialist League (both of which seceded from the Federation), or the Fabian Society (including briefly the Fabian Parliamentary League). If he wished to remain within the Church of England, he could be active in Stewart Headlam's Christian Socialist Guild of Saint Matthew. A nonconforming Protestant had choices ranging from General Booth's Salvation Army through the stable liberalism of R. J. Campbell at the City Temple to the vaguely religious but socially vigorous idealism of Moncure Conway at South Place Chapel. For more exotic tastes there were the Spiritualists, the Comtist Positivists (two branches), or the Theosophists. Although such a varied list of movements could be assembled in any large city at almost any time, it should be noted that all these groups came into being within a single generation—most of them in the 1880's—and that they were almost without exception vigorously launched and supported.

To label these groups the reform movement, although not wholly inaccurate, would certainly be inadequate. They were all manifestations of the great social, political, and religious causes of the nineteenth century, present as early as the 1840's with the Chartists, which led many persons to abandon their old views of the world. Not all of them had the tough objectivity Shaw gave to his Andrew Undershaft:

> Well, you have made for yourself something that you call a morality or a religion or what not. It doesn't fit the facts. Well, scrap it. Scrap it and get one that does fit. . . . If your old religion broke down yesterday, get a newer and better one for tomorrow.

The "facts" most religions did not fit were, basically, Darwinism, Marxism, and widespread poverty.

Shaw attended meetings of many groups and practiced his public speaking whenever he could, but he refused to align himself with any that were specifically religious or atheistic. He did not hesitate, however, to join, and very nearly dominate, the Fabian Society shortly after its founding in 1884. "All Fabians have their price, which is always the adoption of Fabian measures, no matter by what party," Shaw said later, and in his devotion to socialism he willingly gave lectures, wrote articles, and attended committee meetings for any organization that was helping, for the moment, some Fabian cause. He comments on this work in a paper he read to the assembled representatives of the London and Provincial Fabian societies in 1892, published in *Essays in Fabian Socialism*. In recalling the many exhausting jobs he and the Fabians had done, he pauses to observe:

> A man's socialistic acquisitiveness must be keen enough to make him actually prefer spending two or three nights a week in speaking and debating, or in picking up social information even in the most dingy or scrappy way, to going to the theatre, or dancing or drinking, or even sweethearting, if he is to become a really competent propagandist.[3]

Although Shaw's overt devotion was to Fabian socialism, he realized that the basic issue of the time was religious, and he consciously developed a religion of his own, one to complement his socialism and furnish a higher reason for it. As he wrote in his later years of Ruskin:

> He begins as a painter, a lover of music, a poet and a rhetorician, and presently becomes an economist and sociologist, finally developing sociology and economics into a religion, as all economics and sociology that are worth anything do finally develop.[4]

Shaw might, with the substitution of "dramatist" for "poet," have been speaking of himself.

Shaw's first attempt to present his beliefs in an organized pattern was made in the speech "The Religion of the British Empire," given at the City Temple in 1906. The question of how and when he arrived at these tenets from his professed atheism of the 1880's may never be fully answered. That he passed through the religious, political, and economic upheavals of the period with unique detachment is evident, however, for although he adopted ideas from many sources, his religion was, as with his other creations, a unique work of art.

Evidence exists that before 1900 Shaw had ceased to regard himself as an atheist and was carefully examining his beliefs. He said later that he had called himself an atheist "because belief in God then meant belief in the old tribal idol called Jehovah; and I would not, by calling myself an Agnostic, pretend I did not know whether it existed or not." [5]

In an article written in 1888 under the name Shendar Brwa, Shaw pretended to be a foreign visitor, previously ignorant of Christianity and completely confused by the lack of agreement among the British on the meaning of it.[6] In 1895, Shaw wrote to F. H. Evans: "I want to write a big book of devotion for modern people, bringing all the truths latent in the old religious dogmas into contact with real life—a gospel of Shawianity, in fact." [7] In 1896, Shaw published his essay "On Going to Church," in which he attributed most spiritual energies to stimulants or narcotics and recommended for true spiritual regeneration attending a church, but only a beautiful one, and only when there was no service in progress to interrupt worship.[8]

Shaw's most direct encounter with atheism was in a speech he gave before the National Secular Society after Bradlaugh's death. The incident, which probably occurred in the late 1890's or early 1900's, is recounted by Shaw in "Modern Religion I" in this book. It was perhaps natural for the secularists to regard Shaw as a possible successor to Bradlaugh, but apparently they had not been following his career very carefully when they asked him to speak. His topic, "Progress in Free Thought," indicated that he assumed a position existed for the freethinker in advance of Bradlaugh's, but they were not prepared to hear what must have been his frank report on mysticism, in which he used such terms as "Immaculate Conception" and "Trinity." It mattered little that his usage was highly unorthodox. That he should deal with mystical matters at all was too great a shock for those Shaw called "the fundamentalists of the atheistic movement."

The best and most subtle evidence of the maturation of Shaw's religious thought is found in his plays. The first four

(*Widowers' Houses, The Philanderer, Mrs. Warren's Profession,*
and *Arms and the Man*) are concerned primarily with social and
moral questions without reliance upon mystical qualities as
such. The next six (*Candida, The Man of Destiny, You Never
Can Tell, The Devil's Disciple, Caesar and Cleopatra,* and
Captain Brassbound's Conversion) all contain indications that
certain forces beyond rational explanation are at work in guiding human destinies. In addition to the secret in Marchbanks'
heart, Napoleon's "star," and the Devil's Disciple's "My life for
the world's future!" there is the great force, perhaps the most
purely joyous force in all of Shaw, that sweeps the characters of
You Never Can Tell into the twentieth century and culminates
in a basic repudiation of rationalism:

> BOHUN: All matches are unwise. It's unwise to be born;
> it's unwise to be married; it's unwise to live; and it's wise to
> die.
>
> WAITER: Then, if I may respectfully put a word in, sir, so
> much the worse for wisdom!

Caesar and Cleopatra and *Captain Brassbound's Conversion* have
less of the mystical quality than the others, but Caesar does re-
flect the same sure instincts as the Man of Destiny, and Lady
Cicely's authority over Brassbound has a source beyond normal
feminine charm.

Of particular interest in this group of plays, the last written
in 1899, is the character of James Mavor Morell in *Candida*. A
good case can be made for the theory that he was drawn directly
from the figure of Stewart Headlam since, according to the
opening directions, Morell is "a Christian Socialist clergyman of
the Church of England, and an active member of the Guild of
St. Matthew and of the Christian Social Union." Even a copy of
the *Church Reformer,* Headlam's own paper, is on Morell's desk.
Shaw said, however, "I knew practically all the leading Christian
Socialist clergymen. The nearest to Morell was Stopford Brooke,
with touches of Canon Shuttleworth and Fleming Williams." [9]
The creation of a good dramatic character is of course very often
a synthesis, and the references to Headlam seem far too obvious
for a playwright like Shaw to have drawn Morell directly from

him. It is more interesting to assume that Morell represents for Shaw the strengths and weaknesses of the Christian Socialist movement. Although Shaw could not have been a Christian Socialist simply because he could not have been a Christian, he recognized the difficulty of doing God's will without the aftertaste of self-righteousness and complacency. Like Morell, Shaw preached socialist sermons and was the subject of the feminine adulation Candida calls "Prossy's complaint." Bertha Newcombe's well-known portrait, *G. B. S., Platform Spellbinder,* painted in 1893, is so romantically worshipful of its subject that Shaw himself appended: *Portrait by Bertha Newcombe, Spellbound.*[10]

After 1900, Shaw's religious ideas emerge much more strongly in his plays. In *Man and Superman, John Bull's Other Island,* and *Major Barbara,* the mystical forces are confidently recognized for what they are. *Man and Superman* must be regarded as a major opus, including as it does one of Shaw's most significant prefaces, the Don Juan in Hell sequence, and the Revolutionist's Handbook. The preface is an artistic-philosophic creed and a vigorous declaration of independence for the theater of philosophic ideas: "What I have always wanted is a pit of philosophers; and this is a play for such a pit." [11] John Tanner in the play talks of the life-force rather than God, but in *John Bull's Other Island,* through the character of the defrocked priest, Peter Keegan, Shaw gives interpretations of heaven and hell, of penance and redemption. Possibly in conceiving Keegan, Shaw learned that the old religious concepts could be made meaningful when placed in proper perspective against the real world. In *Major Barbara,* with genuine admiration for the vitality of the Salvation Army, he faced religion with the great social problems of poverty and war. Some critics complain that the play is not satisfyingly resolved, not realizing that Shaw united form and content so completely that, given the problem of the play, honest resolution was impossible.

The year after Shaw wrote *Major Barbara,* he delivered the first of the speeches in this book. He was then 50, and his religious ideas were fully formed. His religion was a long time in developing, but it proved durable.

According to Blanche Patch, his secretary in his later years, Shaw never wrote out his speeches, although he prepared meticulously for them and often made copious notes which he did not take to the lecture platform. A man of carefully and consciously developed habits, Shaw carried on in later life what he had trained himself to do in his more active years as a speaker.

Shaw's refusal to write out his speeches indicates that he realized a spoken style should never be the same as a written one. A performer always, he wanted to play upon his audience, utilizing their laughter, judging for himself the duration and intensity of their attention, varying his tempo and attack accordingly, but never as a mere entertainer. He spoke with high purpose.

Fortunately, the reporting of his major speeches was rarely handled casually. They were occasionally taken down stenographically, and when not, they were often reported with extreme faithfulness to detail and style. A reporter for the *Christian Commonwealth,* covering Shaw's City Temple speech of 1906, has effectively preserved the appearance of the lecturer in his prime:

> A little uncommon without being startling . . . rather tall, fair, and bearded, he was attired in a dark suit, a white turn-down collar, and a meek sort of tie. He uses pince-nez which for most of the evening dangled in front of his double-breasted, close-buttoned jacket. His voice is a little metallic, but not unpleasing, his enunciation is very distinct, with barely a suspicion of Irish accent.

R. B. Suthers wrote in the *Clarion* of the audience response when Shaw spoke on "Some Necessary Repairs to Religion" to the Christian Socialist Guild of Saint Matthew two weeks later:

> You can get a tooth drawn for five shillings, with gas, and judging from the torture suffered by a number of people present, I should think they would have preferred to have a tooth drawn, without gas, than to have their cherished religious convictions torn out by the author of *You Never Can Tell.*
>
> There was no anesthetic property in Mr. Shaw's "gas." He used a well-worn pair of forceps, and they hurt. I was sitting at right angles to most of the patients, and I could

see their faces. They were an interesting study, so fascinating that at times they captured my whole attention and I missed one or two of the lecturer's brilliant coruscations.

One man literally squirmed in his seat. His facial muscles were twisted, his teeth ground together, his hands nervously gripped his coat. And yet he seemed to feel that the dentist was quite right. The tooth was a bad one. It must come out.

One dear old lady nodded her head in dissent for an hour. An old man sat and glared with an expression of gloom which gradually deepened into despair. A jovial young man tried to assume an air of smiling, good-natured contempt, but the smile went all awry at times. His tooth had begun to ache. I felt sorry for the people, although the experience will do them good.

The Guild of Saint Matthew speech is nowhere reported fully enough for inclusion in this book, but a *Christian Commonwealth* reporter noted a similar response to "Christianity and Equality," given at the City Temple on October 30, 1913:

More than once the audience sat still and breathless, fascinated by his quite terrifying earnestness and by the merciless vigor of his attack upon the dearest delusions and pretences by which we buttress our self-esteem. The light, patronizing laughter with which half-educated people receive Mr. Shaw's attempts to shock them out of their deadly moral complacency was not heard at the City Temple. The atmosphere was inimical to laughter. And the sight of his tall, tense figure in the pulpit, electrical in its suggestion of vital energy completely under the control of his will—even his beard of flax (to use Richard Middleton's phrase) has a peculiar quality of liveness—compelled a similar intensity of interest and attention from his hearers. Laxity, either of mind or body, is impossible when Mr. Shaw is speaking. Several times I looked round upon my fellow-auditors to mark the effect of his words. I saw consternated faces, hostile faces, faces which bore an expression of alarm and even horror, but not one suggesting boredom or mere tolerance of an inexplicable perversity on the part of the speaker.

Not all of the texts in this book represent the speeches exactly as they were delivered. Shaw himself may have edited some of them for publication, but generally they seem to retain the atmosphere of the public meeting rather than the study—they are less guarded, more unresolved. The reader of Shaw's argumentative prose (as in *The Intelligent Woman's Guide to Socialism and Capitalism*) is often annoyed by the regularity with which Shaw seems to read his mind and have ready in the next paragraph a complete rebuttal to an argument he has scarcely formulated. Even though exasperation at this feat eventually turns to admiration, the image of an intelligence that is almost unfairly superhuman remains. To such annoyance Shaw's speeches are a welcome corrective. He is still there with the same arguments, but he seems more friendly. He wanders from the point, repeats himself, fails to complete his logic, and is in other ways more human. He is still irrefutable, but he is at least not unassailable.

Shaw spoke on many different subjects but used every opportunity to promote Fabian socialism, to which he often joined his doctrine of creative evolution after it was formulated. Nearly all of his speeches tended to become political and religious, but relatively few set out to deal specifically with the problems of modern religion. Only major addresses were permanently recorded, and few of his off-the-cuff remarks, such as those in "What Irish Protestants Think," which present him at his most spontaneous, have been preserved. Since the collecting of Shaviana is currently fashionable, other religious speeches may be uncovered, but this book contains all for which reasonably complete texts exist, including those customarily referred to by Shaw's biographers and those casually mentioned in newspapers and periodicals. Speeches for which only scattered fragments of text exist are not included. Especially unfortunate is the lack of adequate versions of the important speeches Shaw gave before the National Secular Society and the Guild of Saint Matthew.

The speeches in this book may seem repetitious at times, but the reader must remember that although the audiences changed from 1906 to 1937, Shaw continued to pursue the same subjects. His favorite story of pulling out his watch and giving the Almighty five minutes to strike him dead may lose its effect after three repetitions, but preachers are repetitious by definition. They have one gospel and spend their lives spreading it. Shaw was no exception.

Once formulated, Shaw's religious ideas changed very little, but he never wrote the "gospel of Shawianity" he proposed in 1895. The preface to *Back to Methuselah* is a textbook on creative evolution developed from the ideas expressed in the preface to *Man and Superman* seventeen years before. The preface to *Androcles and the Lion* and the preface to *On the Rocks,* written twenty years later, both critically examine the bases of Christianity. The preface to *Saint Joan* deals with mysticism and sainthood. In the parable *The Adventures of the Black Girl in Her Search for God,* Shaw's heroine finds all the available gods false or unsatisfactory and chooses to settle down in Voltaire's garden with a somewhat boorish, though hardworking, red-bearded Irish socialist. "What Is My Religious Faith?" in *Sixteen Self Sketches* and Shaw's preface to Richard Albert Wilson's *The Miraculous Birth of Language*[12] are religious statements made when Shaw was in his nineties and contain no surprises. In the preface to *Farfetched Fables,* written in the last year of his life, Shaw remained content to use the term "divine providence," or simply "providence," as an acceptable synonym for the life-force.

Time and experience, even the European debacle of 1914–1918, which profoundly challenged Shaw's notions of human progress, did not materially alter his religious philosophy, expressed in its simplest and most direct form in the first speeches in this book. His beliefs can be summarized briefly as follows:

> Religion is a necessity. A divine purpose must be recognized in the universe. Life as a haphazard accident in the evolutionary process is too horrible to contemplate.
>
> All present-day institutional religions are unsatisfactory. Though much of Jesus' personal theology is sound, no modern state would permit it to be put into practice. Institutional Christianity is a failure because the Christian church is still caught between the Old Testament horror gods and the intimidating salvationism of St. Paul.
>
> True religion is always mystical. It is carried on by prophets, not priests. The true protestant renounces all churches and all priesthoods.
>
> Religion must be practical. It must concern itself with justice and economics and the social order and the divine value of human life—not otherworldliness—but sheer pragmatism as a rule of life cannot be tolerated. A practice is not right simply because it can be made to work.

God is not an omnipotent personality, but a blind life-force, struggling through evolution and whatever other means are available to it to develop what one day might be the Godhead. "He's not properly made and finished yet." (*The Adventures of the Black Girl in Her Search for God*) The so-called natural selection of Darwinism reduces this force to chance or accident, thereby, as Samuel Butler has pointed out, banishing mind from the universe.

The life-force has a will of its own, and its will is in man—perhaps in all living things. Men of genius are conscious of this purpose and try to help it along. Ordinary men may be doing its will unconsciously, but the true joy in life is in the knowledge of being used for a purpose mightier and larger than selfish desires for happiness.

The life-force needs man to carry out its purposes. It needs his hands and his brains. If he does not do well enough, it will eventually have to scrap him and develop a more advanced species. "We must drive into the heads of men the full consciousness of moral responsibility that comes with the knowledge that there will never be a God unless we make him." ("The Religion of the Future")

For the origin of these ideas, Shaw took pains to acknowledge his debt to, among others, Bunyan, Bergson, Butler, Bradlaugh, Shelley, Ibsen, Voltaire, and the writers of the Gospels. In Shaw's hands, however, the doctrine of creative evolution and the life-force approaches the stature of an original theology.

Much of Shaw's effectiveness as a religious lecturer came from his ability to sound disarmingly orthodox and shockingly radical at the same time. A section from almost any of his religious speeches could be placed in a sermon in almost any church without violating the sermon's context; yet there is no doubt that his utterances are truly heretical. They were when he made them, and they still are. Although the orthodoxies of Christianity have become less confining since Shaw's time, he could still ask, "Where in the world is there a Church that will receive me on such terms, or into which I could honestly consent to be received?" [13] The world continues to acclaim him as an entertainer, but it still recoils from his full message.

WARREN SYLVESTER SMITH

Lemont, Pennsylvania
May 27, 1963

✳xxiii

THE RELIGIOUS SPEECHES OF
BERNARD SHAW

✳✳✳✳✳✳✳✳✳✳

THE RELIGION OF
THE BRITISH EMPIRE

✳✳✳✳ This lecture was delivered at the City Temple on November 22, 1906, and reported in the *Christian Commonwealth* on November 29. Sections of the report obviously in Shaw's style of direct address but not enclosed in quotation marks have been restored here to first person. (A similar procedure has been followed in "The Religion of the Future" and "Christianity and Equality.") The words within brackets here and in the speeches that follow are, unless otherwise indicated, those of the reporter.

[I confess that my knowledge of Mr. Bernard Shaw, mainly gathered from the newspapers and the reports of his lectures as delivered in Manchester and Birmingham, did not encourage the hope that his appearance at the City Temple would be very satisfactory. Let me at once say that, with one conspicuous exception to which I shall presently refer, Mr. Shaw said little or nothing of a "shocking" character. While his terminology in dealing with grave subjects is of a kind to which old-fashioned people are not accustomed, his attitude to solemn questions was essentially reverent, and, what was undoubtedly a surprise to many of his hearers, he revealed himself to be a man of strong and definite religious conviction.

A more interesting and stimulating evening rarely falls to one's lot. The audience was evidently just as much delighted with Mr. Shaw as he was with it. There may be aspects of Mr. Shaw's personality and he may entertain opinions that would not have been equally pleasing; I confine myself to speaking of him as I found him on Thursday evening.

Introducing the lecturer, Mr. Campbell [1] said he believed that underneath his witticisms and paradoxes and even whimsicalities there was a serious purpose, though he questioned whether Mr. Shaw could be got to acknowledge that. Probably every hearer would agree that the first part of Mr. Campbell's remark was abundantly sustained by the lecture that followed. Not a few of the audience had evidently come expecting to be enjoyably shocked and titillated and entertained throughout, but it seemed to me that Mr. Shaw rarely, if at all, yielded to the inevitable temptation to say unusual or paradoxical or daring things merely for the fun of saying them or being thought smart or clever. He said them because they came naturally to him, and because he believed them.]

✳

I begin with a remark that might go without saying, though perhaps, remembering the place in which I speak, it is as well to make it clear that nobody but myself is responsible for what I say. My first proposition is that you can't have an Empire without a religion, and my next that if the Empire is to be a real thing all the people in it must believe the same truth—though it does not matter what legends they accept or what imagery they use.

✳

[Mr. Shaw then read from the *Statesman's Year Book* the lengthy list of the nominal religions of the British Empire, finishing up with the Peculiar People, "who literally believe in the Bible as a rule of life." The Protestant sects outside the Established Church were grouped under the general heading of Voltairean sects, most leaders of the Free Churches, e.g., Dr. Clifford and Mr. Silvester Horne,[2] according to Mr. Shaw, holding opinions that were held by Voltaire. Mr. Shaw hastened to repudiate the idea that Voltaire was an atheist, and, in view of the celebrated Frenchman's splendid record of social work, his farsightedness, his self-sacrificing philanthropy, urged that Free Churchmen should set up busts of Voltaire in all their places of worship.

Illustrating the curious political predicament brought about by the necessity of making laws in order to prevent riots being caused by people recklessly offending the religious susceptibilities of others, Mr. Shaw mentioned that in India we prosecute a Christian who endangers the public peace by denouncing Mohammedanism or Brahmanism, and in the Sudan we punish people for selling the Bible in the streets of Khartoum. This led him to make fine sport of passive resisters who go to prison rather than pay for Anglican teaching at the very same time when they are maintaining the Roman Catholic Church in Malta. . . . Mr. Shaw's solution of the "religious question" is that members of a state must tolerate one another's sects or religions and be willing to contribute to some extent towards the support of them.

Then came an allusion to Ibsen, a "very great religious force in the nineteenth century," and a quotation from *Brand* ("the history of a deeply religious man") of the striking passage in which the titular character protests, "I do not believe in your God. Your God is an old man, my God is a young man."]

✱

We are apt to picture God as an elderly gentleman with a beard, whereas he ought to be typified as an eternally young man. It is from the great poet, who is always the really religious man, that we get true ideas on great subjects. Matthew Arnold said that most Englishmen's idea of the Trinity was three Lord Shaftesburys.[3]

Let me define for you a religious man as I see him: He is a very rare being, and sometimes a very dangerous one, but he is a man who has a constant sense, amounting on his part to a positive knowledge, that he is only the instrument of a power which is a universal power, the power that created the universe and brought it into being, that he is not in the world for his own narrow purposes, but that he is the instrument of that power.

Given that belief, it is of no consequence what else a man might hold; without it, a man has no religion in him. The great tragedy of human character is human cowardice. We pretend that we are brave men, but the reason why a nation will allow nothing to be said against its courage is because it knows it has none. Without fear we could not live a single day; if you were not afraid of being run over, you would be run over before you got home. What will really nerve a man, what, as history has shown over and over again, will turn a coward into a brave man, is the belief that he is the instrument of a larger and higher power. What he makes of this conviction and the power it gives depends upon his brain or conscience.

There are people who imagine that they have apologized for everything when they say, "I did my best. I acted according to my conscience." But that is not enough. The one thing you will never get in this life is any simple rule of conduct that will get you through life. From that point of view I ventured the other day in Manchester to criticize the idea—it is the idea of the old Pharisees—of those people who think they have done everything when they have kept the Ten Commandments. I insisted that that did not get them a bit further in the direction of refinement. That is the specially Christian point of view, no discovery of mine, and yet when I uttered this old commonplace of Christianity, the Bishop of Manchester almost went into fits, denounced me in unmeasured terms for having ventured to deny that you can make the keeping of the commandments, and so on, a quite sufficient rule of life: whereas I was perfectly easily able to show, as I could show you tonight, that almost all the commandments, with perhaps two exceptions, are commandments which we ought very frequently to break as a simple matter of public and private duty.

✳

[This cryptic utterance . . . was the hard saying of the lecture, and it was a pity Mr. Shaw did not pause to make clear precisely what he meant, as probably he could have given an explanation that would have been perfectly satisfactory to his hearers.]

✳

One of the difficulties of really able and earnest ministers of religion in this country is that they cannot get their own congregations to understand how little difference there is between them and other persons who belong to other sects and congregations. I have never had any difficulty whatever in getting on with religious people; it is the irreligious people that I can't get on with. If I write a play, and critics begin to rave about my mocking at religion and my bad taste, you will find that the notice does not breathe the spirit of religion, and that the writer, though he may be a very clever and honest man, has not the slightest idea of what religion means. Furthermore, he represents a very widespread feeling in this country that any man who makes an attempt to apply religion to the actual affairs of life ought to be suppressed.

The average man of today knows and admits that he has religious duties, and he knows that if they are taken seriously they conflict very seriously with his daily practice in business.

Therefore he says, "I can't always be bothering with religion, I have certain religious duties, but I can't always be attending to them, and therefore I want to have a particular day set apart to keep it holy. I will do all my business on the six days and all my religion on the seventh, and then they will never come into conflict. You make that arrangement, and I will come down handsome, and build your churches and pay your stipends and keep things going for you." For myself, I like to have a little religion every day of my life. I may not keep Sunday holy in such a tremendous manner as the ordinary city man does, but then I don't altogether secularize Monday and the other days. I find life goes on best when I spread my religion over all the week.

The religious life is a happy life. Because I do not eat meat and drink whisky, people think I am an ascetic. I am not. I am a voluptuary! I avoid eating meat because it is a nasty thing to eat; I avoid drinking whisky because it gives me unpleasant and disagreeable sensations. I want to live the pleasantest sort of life I possibly can. What I like is not what people call pleasure, which is the most dreadful and boring thing on the face of the earth, but life itself. And that of course is the genuinely religious view to take, because life is a very wonderful thing. Life is this force outside yourself that you are in the hands of. You must not forget that the ordinary man who is not religious, who does not know that he is an instrument in the hands of the higher power, is nevertheless such an instrument all the time.

While I have been describing the religious man you have been saying, "That's me!" and while I have been describing the irreligious man you have been saying, "That's Jones!" But I don't want you to feel uncharitable towards Jones. Although only an agricultural laborer, Jones may be doing the work of the universe in a more efficient way than the man who has become conscious of the higher power and brought his own mind to bear upon it, but not having a first-rate mind, and being mixed up with purely rationalistic theories of the universe, he may be doing a great deal of mischief, doing something to defeat the higher power. For it is possible to defeat that power, as I shall presently show.

Any personal belief is a document, at any rate. You may think mine fantastic, even paradoxical. I have more or less swallowed all the formulas, I have been in all the churches, studied all the religions with a great deal of sympathy, and I will tell you where I have come out. Most people call this great force in the universe God. I am not very fond of this form myself, because it is a little too personal, too close to the idea of the elderly gentleman with the beard. But we won't quarrel about the term. To me the higher power is something larger than a personal force. But even the people who would agree with me there still cling to the idea that it is an almighty force, that it is a force which can directly and immediately do what it likes. But if so, why in the name of common sense did he make such creatures as you and I? If he wants his will fulfilled on earth, why did he put himself in the position of having to have that will fulfilled by our actions? Because what is done in this world has to be done by us.

We know that a lot of work lies before us. What we call civilization has landed us in horrible iniquities and injustices. We have got to get rid of them, and it has to be done by us. There is the dilemma. Why is it not done by God? I believe God, in the popular acceptance of the word, to be completely powerless. I do not believe that God has any hands or brain of our kind. What I know he has, or rather is, is will. But will is useless without hands and brain.

Then came a process which we call evolution. I do not mean natural selection as popularized by Charles Darwin. He did not discover or even popularize evolution; on the contrary, he drove evolution out of men's minds for half a century, and we have only just got it back again. The general doctrine of evolution shows how, out of a perfectly amorphous form of life, something which we picture to ourselves as a little speck of protoplasm in a wonderful way by constant effort and striving evolved higher and higher forms of life, until gradually you have a thing so comparatively wonderful as men and women. That evolutionary process to me is God: this wonderful will of the universe, struggling and struggling, and bit by bit making hands and brains for himself, feeling that, having this will, he must also have material organs with which to grapple with material things. And that is the reason we have come into existence.

If you don't do his work it won't be done; if you turn away

from it, if you sit down and say, "Thy will be done," you might as well be the most irreligious person on the face of the earth. But if you will stand by your God, if you will say, "My business is to do your will, my hands are your hands, my tongue is your tongue, my brain is your brain, I am here to do thy work, and I will do it," you will get rid of otherworldliness, you will get rid of all that religion which is made an excuse and a cloak for doing nothing, and you will learn not only to worship your God, but also to have a fellow feeling with him.

✳

[Mr. Shaw added that he had to choose between the two conceptions: a God who might have made a happy world and deliberately did not do it, and the benevolent will he had described, resulting in the realization of God in man—not a metaphysical conception, but the Word becoming flesh.]

✳

This conception that I am doing God's work in the world gives me a certain self-satisfaction—not with the limitations of my power and the extravagances of my brain or hand—but a certain self-respect and force in the world. People like their religion to be what they call comforting. I want my religion to give me self-respect and courage, and I can do without comfort, without happiness, without everything else. This sort of faith really overcomes the power of death.

This brings me to my last heresy. I never can really respect a religion which postulates the ordinary conception of a personal immortality. You have not overcome the fear of death until you delight in your own life, believing it to be the carrying-out of the universal purpose, until you are perfectly ready to let the life that is in your brain and hand go into another brain and hand, and no longer cling to your miserable individual life.

I do not want to try and drag you to that point tonight. I have only been trying to show you one or two landmarks as they appear to me. I do not ask you to agree. I need not ask you to be shocked; if a speaker is sincere, an audience never is shocked. [*Applause*] I have offered you my own living convictions for what they are worth. I only ask you to think about them, and I think you will admit that, leaving out details, the spirit of what I have said is the spirit in which perhaps all the really effective men in the Empire and in the world are working together at the present time, and in that working together we have some real hope for the future of humanity.

*

[A burst of enthusiastic applause followed the conclusion of this remarkable lecture. Mr. Campbell said he was absolutely at one with Mr. Shaw in nearly all that he had said. He could not help thinking of God as more than a continuously persistent will. "I think of God as the universal consciousness, and of that consciousness as infinite and eternal. I think of space and time as being more or less illusions, and I think of this limited universe as God's deliberately sought opportunity for self-expression— there I am on common ground with Mr. Shaw. The reason for that self-expression of God appears to me to be this: The ideal life, the highest plane of existence of which you can form any conception, however vague, is love. Love to realize itself must know sacrifice; sacrifice implies limitation; hence the universe, with its struggle and pain and seeming failure, the horror and darkness of it all." On the question of immortality, Mr. Campbell said, "To me the really difficult thing to believe is that we shall ever stop. Eternity cannot be time *plus* time *plus* time *ad infinitum*. If our consciousness could only get outside or above the limitation we might see that we never began. For if we are essential to the being of God, if we are so to speak contained in it, nothing that has ever existed can possibly cease to exist, because it is present to the all-embracing consciousness of God. I can imagine this limited fragmentary spark of a consciousness that each of us possesses being fulfilled in the eternal being of God, but I cannot imagine it being destroyed."

A vote of thanks having been carried with acclamation, Mr. Shaw said in the course of a brief response that religion is the most interesting thing in the world. When he was a dramatic critic he often wondered at people paying half a guinea to sit in uncomfortable stalls, to listen to bad music, and see something frightfully dull, when by going to the City Temple or Westminster Abbey or St. Paul's and paying less money they could get a much more comfortable seat, hear much better music, and listen to much more interesting talk.

There may be many Bernard Shaws, but the one who appeared at the City Temple last Thursday night completely won the hearts of his audience and made himself a host of friends.]

THE NEW THEOLOGY

✳✳✳✳   These notes for a lecture Shaw gave at Kensington
Town Hall on May 16, 1907, were printed in the
Christian Commonwealth on May 23 and 30 and
in shortened form in the *Los Angeles Examiner*
on July 21.

Shaw apparently refers in the first sentence to a
speech delivered before the Guild of Saint Matthew at Essex Hall on November 29, 1906. This
speech, "Some Necessary Repairs to Religion," was,
according to the *Times* of November 30, essentially the same as "The Religion of the British
Empire" (*qv.*).

Stewart Headlam, who sponsored the Essex Hall
appearance, was vigorously criticized for engaging
Shaw to speak at a Guild function. The Bishop
of London demanded and got Headlam's formal
repudiation "of the statements in Mr. Bernard
Shaw's lecture, which were in contradiction to
the Christian faith."

When I last stood on this platform, I said there was not a single
established religion in the world in which an intelligent or educated man could believe. Some feeling has been shown by those
who have quoted that statement that somehow or other it is my
fault, and I am not altogether disposed to deny it. A person who
points out a thing of which the mass of people are unconscious
really does to some extent create the thing which he points out.
I remember not very long ago rolling up my sleeves to the
elbow in order to wash my hands, and, as I have a great deal
to think about, including the New Theology, I am sometimes
rather absent minded. The consequence was that I forgot to
roll down my sleeves, and walked about two miles in the west of
London until I met a friend, who said, "What on earth are you
going about in that fashion for?" Now, as I did not know that

my sleeves were rolled up, they were not rolled up so far as I was concerned until that intrusive friend came and quite unnecessarily called my attention to the fact, covering me with blushes and confusion. And so my remark here last year may have destroyed the authenticity of established religions for many persons who up to that moment had believed that those religions, being established, were all right.

I want to see whether there is any possibility of our arriving at a religion on which we can agree, because it is very important we should have a religion of some kind. I know that that is quite a fashionable opinion, but we have got out of the habit of thinking that we ought to believe in the religion we have. Hardly any person in London believes in the religion he professes. Now let us come to the New Theology.[1] It is not my habit, nor the habit of any really judicious lecturer, to begin by definitions, and when I do, I decline to be held by them. I do not address myself to your logical faculties, but as one human mind trying to put himself in contact with other human minds. By theology I really do mean the science of godhead, and I want to examine whether we have made any advance in the science, whether there is a science of it in which we can believe and on which we can get a pretty general agreement. I shall have to go back a considerable distance, because I want to make you aware of the state of your mind on the question. I am quite certain that you do not know it, unless you are familiar with the religious history of the nineteenth century, perhaps the wickedest in all human history.

When I came to London, at about the beginning of the last quarter of the nineteenth century, I found people in a very curious state as regards their religious belief. This was illustrated by something that happened at a bachelor party I attended in Kensington not far from this hall a short time after I arrived. I found myself in the company of a number of young men who either belonged to, or were qualifying for, one of the liberal professions, and they got into a dispute about religion. At that time the late Charles Bradlaugh[2] was very notorious for the militant campaign he was carrying on as an atheist. One of the persons present, representing what was supposed to be the pious and religious side in the controversy, accused Bradlaugh of having publicly taken out his watch and challenged the Almighty, if he had the power and will to do so, to strike him dead in five minutes. An admirer and adherent of Bradlaugh vehemently denied that story, saying it was a gross calumny. The gentleman who made the accusation took the old-fashioned view; it had prevailed in this country for about three hundred years, that very dark period in which Christians, instead of being Christians in any reasonable sense, worshiped the Bible as a talisman. For instance, in tract shops you saw copies of the Bible exhibited with the dent of a bullet in them, and you were given to understand that the soldier who had in his pocket a testament given him by his mother had been saved from death because the book had stopped the enemy's bullet. The gentleman who told the story about Mr. Bradlaugh was a Bible worshiper, and believed, among other things, the story in the Bible that when Elisha the prophet was mocked because of his bald head by some young children, God sent a couple of bears out of a wood to eat those children.[3] And the extraordinary thing is that the gentleman worshiped the God who did that! If you or I confessed doing such a thing as that probably we should be torn to pieces. But it was a common article of belief at that time that the universe was ruled by a God who was that particular sort of person, an exceedingly spiteful person, capable of taking the most ferocious revenge.

I was very much puzzled by the impassioned way in which the gentleman who was a secularist defended Charles Bradlaugh against the imputation of having taken out his watch and made this challenge, and when my turn came to speak, or rather when I spoke—I am not always in the habit of waiting for my turn exactly—I said that if the question which Charles Bradlaugh was dealing with was whether a God of that kind existed, the reported experiment seemed to me perfectly legitimate and natural and to deny the existence of such a God appeared to me to be a far more genuine religious position than that of the people who affirmed belief in him. I say it seemed to me perfectly natural and proper, if the ruler of the universe were really the petty, spiteful criminal he was represented to be, for a man who denied his existence to take his watch out of his pocket and, instead of troubling about what happened many centuries ago, to ask him to strike him dead at the end of five minutes. I said, "Since it appears that Mr. Bradlaugh never made this experiment, I, regarding it as a perfectly legitimate one, will try it myself," and with that I took my watch out of my pocket.

I have never done anything in public or private which produced such an instantaneous and extraordinary effect. Up to that moment the company had been divided into a pious and a sceptical party, but it now appeared that there were no sceptics present at all. Everyone of them felt it to be extremely probable that before the five minutes were up I should be taken at my word. One of the party appealed to us to turn the conversation to a more lively channel, and a gentleman present who had a talent for singing comic songs sat down at the piano and sang the most melancholic comic song I ever heard in my life.

That incident has its amusing side, but it also has its tragic side. It is a frightful thing that it should have been possible so recently as twenty-five years ago for a party of educated men to be in that state of superstition. I am not at all certain that I have not made some of those I address very uncomfortable by what I have just said. Well, I intend to go on making people who hold such views uncomfortable. I want to make them understand in a very vivid way that it is quite impossible at this time of day to unite the world or appeal to our highest intelligence or better natures by preaching that particular sort of God. It was the preaching of that kind of tribal idol that accounted for Charles Bradlaugh calling himself an atheist, and, disbelieving with my whole soul in such a being, I always did what Charles Bradlaugh did: made myself intelligible to those people who worship such a monster by saying that I was an atheist. And in that sense I still am an atheist, as it must seem to me every humane person must be. That kind of God is morally inconceivable. The God who would send bears to eat up little children would be a wicked God—what Shelley called an Almighty Fiend. Why did not Shelley's protest produce very much impression on the people of this country? Because, believing he was an Almighty Fiend, they feared and obeyed him very largely as such and supposed that if they told him the truth to his face he would probably strike them dead for blasphemy. They saw that there was a great deal of terrible cruelty in the world, which rather confirmed the idea that the force at the back of things was wicked and cruel, and therefore the denunciations of Shelley and others of the current conception of God as immoral did not remove the presumption that he existed.

There was another reason why these people had to believe in God: Everywhere in nature they saw evidence of design. It was no use telling them the universe was the result of blind chance. They said, "If you look around, if you note all that we are told even by scientific men about the marvelous adaptation of means to end, if you consider such a miraculous thing as the human eye, it is impossible for us to believe that these things came into existence without a designer, and we cannot blind ourselves to the fact that the designer is apparently cruel. We see plague, pestilence, and famine, battle, murder, and sudden death; we see our parents dying of cancer, our children dying of diphtheria. We may not dare to say that the power that wills that is cruel; it might bring worse consequences on us. But the cruelty is no reason for our ceasing to believe in its existence." And so, neither science on the one hand, nor the moral remonstrances of Shelley and his school on the other, were able to shake the current belief in that old theology that came back to the old tribal idol, Jehovah.

I hope that I have produced a sufficiently gloomy impression upon you! The reason I have been putting the matter as I have is that I want to bring into your minds very strongly the fact that in the middle of the last century all the mind, conscience, and intelligence of the best part of mankind was in revolt against the old-fashioned conception of God, and yet at the same time finding itself intellectually unable to get away from the conception of God the Designer. They were in a dilemma. There must be what they called God, and yet they could not make him responsible for the good in the world without making him also responsible for the evil, because they never questioned one thing about him: that, being the designer of the universe, he must be necessarily omnipotent. This being the situation, is it not clear that if at that time any man had risen up and said, "All this wonderful adaptation of means to end, all this design which seems to imply a designer, is an illusion; it may have all come about by the operation of what we call blind chance," the most intelligent and best part of the human race, without stopping to criticize his argument very closely, would spring at that man and take him to their arms as their moral savior, saying, "You have lifted from our minds this horrible conception that the force that is governing us all and is managing the whole world is hideous, criminal, cruel"? That is exactly what happened when Charles Darwin appeared and the reason why he had such an enormous success that the religion of the last half of the nineteenth century became Darwinian. Many people are under the impression that Darwinism meant that the world had been converted to a belief in evolution. That is a mistake; exactly the contrary has happened. Darwin was really the man who completely turned the attention of mankind from the doctrine of evolution.

Evolution is a vital part of the New Theology, but it sprang into something like completeness as a conception at the end of the eighteenth century, when all the great evolutionists, including Erasmus Darwin, grandfather of Charles Darwin, brought out their books and developed the whole system. The main thing by which they astonished the world was by attacking the old conception of creation in the Garden of Eden. The amazing conception that thought of all life on this planet as having evolved from a little speck of slime in a ditch struck the world dumb. Erasmus Darwin justified the theology of it by saying, "Is not the conception that men have been developed from a speck of protoplasm much more wonderful than that the world and everything in it was made in six days?" The conception took hold of people, and its chief exponent was the great philosopher Lamarck,[4] a Frenchman who began life as a soldier and ended it as a naturalist. In one of his books Lamarck gave an illustration of the process of evolution. He said the reason that the giraffe had a long neck is that this creature wanted to feed on the soft herbage on the top of tall trees, and by dint of generations of giraffes stretching their necks, they gradually made their necks longer, until they could reach the requisite height. Now, that means that the giraffe got a long neck because it wanted a long neck—just in the same way that you learn to ride a bicycle or to speak French because you want to do so.

Well, in the year 1830, the scientific world got tired of gen-

the guess — shaw juxtuposes

RELIGIOUS SPEECHES OF BERNARD SHAW

eralizing and, instead of forming great cosmic theories, devoted itself to the study of isolated phenomena, assisted by the microscope, and shortly after this time Charles Darwin came on the scene. I am convinced that the accusations made against Darwin of having deliberately suppressed the debt that civilization owed to his grandfather for the discovery of evolution were entirely unjust, because I don't believe that Charles Darwin knew anything about evolution, or that to the end of his life he ever understood the whole theory or what it meant. From boyhood he delighted in frogs and pigeons and was the greatest pigeon fancier that ever lived. The real thing that enabled Charles Darwin to come to different conclusions from other naturalists was that between the time of the evolutionists of 1790–1830 and Charles Darwin's discovery in his book, *The Origin of Species*,[5] the researches of the great biologist Lyell [6] led him to teach the world that the stratification and formation of rocks and mountains in order to be scientifically accounted for forced us to assign a much greater age to the earth than had hitherto been assigned. Our grandfathers had always been taught, on the authority of Archbishop Ussher,[7] that the world was 6,006 years old, and some people had actually discovered the actual day of the month when creation began. This present of millions of years gave time for Darwin's theory of natural selection. Now let us apply this theory to the case of the giraffe. Lamarck's theory implied purpose and will, and, remember, if there is purpose and will in a microbe there must be purpose and will through the whole universe. But Darwin said, in effect, "I can explain the giraffe's long neck without implying the slightest purpose or will. What really happened was this: The number of giraffes multiplied until they began to prey on the means of subsistence—until they bit off all the leaves on the trees within their reach, and then they found themselves starving. But supposing, by one of those little accidents and variations that will always occur—we do not know how—a few giraffes happened to have necks a little longer than the others, they would be able to reach vegetation, while their less fortunate fellows starved. Consequently the longer-necked giraffes would survive while the others perished and produce a race of giraffes with necks a little longer, and this without any purpose or design."

*15

My difficulty in putting this apparently commonplace story of the giraffe before a modern audience is to make them understand the unspeakable and frightful prospect opened to the world by Darwin. He abolished adaptation and design, and, as Samuel Butler⁸ said, banished mind from the universe, which was a great relief to many Englishmen who greatly dislike anything in the shape of reflection. Considering that there are and necessarily must be a large number of consciously religious men always living, and that everyone of us has a considerable religious element in him and could not exist without it, why was it that the naked horror of Darwin's conception did not strike them? I have already given you the explanation; it is Elisha and the bears again. The world had got so horrified by the old theology, with its conception of a spiteful, narrow, wicked, personal God, who was always interfering and doing stupid things—often cruel things—that for the moment it could feel nothing but relief at having got rid of such a God altogether. It did not feel the void at first. A man with a bad toothache only thinks of getting rid of the tooth; it is not till afterwards he discovers that he must have a new tooth if he is to go on eating and keep his digestion in order. So people said, "Now that we have got rid of the old conception of religion we will believe in science and evolution." Of course, they knew nothing about evolution; they thought that natural selection, Darwin's discovery, was evolution. Darwin merely turned the attention of mankind to the effects of natural selection; he did not deal with the real problem of evolution. Samuel Butler and others were very soon able to show that it was no use denying the existence of purpose and will in the universe; they were conscious themselves of having purpose, will, design. Then came the discovery of the weak point of the natural selection theory: that it not only did away with the necessity for design and purpose, but with the necessity for consciousness. Men were able to demonstrate that, according to the theory of natural selection, it was perfectly possible that all the books in the British Museum might have been written, all the pictures in the National Gallery might have been painted, all the cathedrals of Europe might have been built, automatically, without one person concerned in the process having been conscious of what he was doing. Some of the natural selectionists used to make the demonstration themselves with a certain pride in doing so. But the common sense of mankind said, "If all the operations of the species can be accounted for without conscious- ness, intelligence, or design, you have still.got to account for the consciousness, intelligence, and design that undoubtedly exist in man." The religious people naturally turn this argument to account, saying, "It is all very well to say that life is a mere pursuit of pleasure and gain, but many men do not live in order to get a balance of pleasure over pain; you see everywhere men doing work that does not benefit them—they call it God's work; natural selection cannot account for that. There is behind the universe an intelligent and driving force of which we ourselves are a part —a divine spark."

After the Darwins and Lyell and Samuel Butler had had their say, the difficulty presented was this: How are we to retain the notion of design without going back to the idea that the design is the work of a cruel designer? The trouble, as usual, was that we had been making the entirely gratuitous assumption that the force behind the universe is omnipotent. Now, you cannot prove that that force is at once omnipotent and benevolent. If omnipotent, why did it create us? If there are three orders of existence—man as we know him, the angels higher than man, and God higher than the angels—why did God first create something lower than himself, the angels, and then actually create something lower than the angels, man? I cannot believe in a God who would do that. If I were God, I should try to create something higher than myself, and then something higher than that, so that, beginning with a God the highest thing in creation, I should end with a God the lowest thing in creation. This is the conception you must get into your head if you are to be free from the horrible old idea that all the cruelty in the world is the work of an omnipotent God, who if he liked could have left the cruelty out of creation, who instead of creating us. . . . Just think about yourselves, ladies and gentlemen. I do not want to be uncomplimentary, but can you conceive God deliberately creating you if he could have created anything better?

What you have got to understand is that somehow or other there is at the back of the universe a will, a life-force. You cannot think of him as a person, you have to think of him as a great purpose, a great will, and, furthermore, you have to think of him as engaged in a continual struggle to produce something higher and higher, to create organs to carry out his purpose; as wanting hands, and saying, "I must create something with hands"; arriving at that very slowly, after innumerable experiments and innumerable mistakes, because this power must be proceeding as we proceed, because if there were any other way it would put us in that way: we know that in all the progress we make we proceed by way of trial and error and experiment. Now conceive of the force behind the universe as a bodiless, impotent force, having no executive power of its own, wanting instruments, something to carry out its will in the world, making all manner of experiments, creating reptiles, birds, animals, trying one thing after another, rising higher and higher in the scale of organism, and finally producing man, and then inspiring that man, putting his will into him, getting him to carry out his purpose, saying to him, "Remember, you are not here merely to look after yourself. I have made your hand to do my work; I have made your brain, and I want you to work with that and try to find out the purpose of the universe; and when one instrument is worn out, I will make another, and another, always more and more intelligent and effective." One difficulty is that so many of the earlier efforts of this world-force—for example, the tiger—remain, and the incompatibility between them and man exists in the human being himself as the result of early experiments, so that there are certain organs in your body which are perishing away and are of no use and actually interfere with your later organs. And here you have, as it seems to me, the explanation of that great riddle which used to puzzle people—evil and pain.

Numbers of things which are at present killing and maiming us in our own organism have got to be evolved out of that organism, and the process is painful. The object of the whole evolutionary process is to realize God; that is to say, instead of the old notion that creation began with a God, a personal being, who, being perfect, created something lower than himself, the aim of the New Theology is to turn that process the other way and to conceive of the force behind the universe as working up through imperfection and mistake to a perfect, organized being, having the power of fulfilling its highest purposes. In a sense there is no God as yet achieved, but there is that force at work making God, struggling through us to become an actual organized existence, enjoying what to many of us is the greatest conceivable ecstasy, the ecstasy of a brain, an intelligence, actually conscious of the whole, and with executive force capable of guiding it to a perfectly benevolent and harmonious end. That is what we are working to. When you are asked, "Where is God? Who is God?" stand up and say, "I am God and here is God, not as yet completed, but still advancing towards completion, just in so much as I am working for the purpose of the universe, working for the good of the whole of society and the whole world, instead of merely looking after my personal ends." In that way we get rid of the old contradiction, we begin to perceive that the evil of the world is a thing that will finally be evolved out of the world, that it was not brought into the world by malice and cruelty, but by an entirely benevolent designer that had not as yet discovered how to carry out its benevolent intention. In that way I think we may turn towards the future with greater hope.

It had been my intention when I began to make the few introductory remarks which I have just delivered the first part of my lecture and then to go on applying that to existing religion, to deal with the actual articles of the Church of England, and to show how much of this truth that I have been teaching tonight is to be found in them. You will find a great deal of this truth in them and in your Bible and in all the religious books of the world. You will find it in the modern poets. When you once seize this you will find that this idea is no idle heresy or paradox of mine, but that it has been germinating in people's minds for a century past and for much more than that in the great poets and leaders of mankind.

THE IDEAL
OF CITIZENSHIP

✳✳✳✳   This address was given before the Progressive
League at the City Temple on October 11, 1909.
R. J. Campbell, who served as chairman, thought
the speech significant enough to place it in the
appendix to the 1909 edition of his book, *The
New Theology* (London: Mills & Boon Ltd.).

Mr. Campbell, Ladies and Gentlemen: I suppose I have addressed as many hopeful progressive leagues as any man in London. I have sampled them nearly all for the last thirty years, but
I think this is the first time I have addressed one in the City
Temple. I have been looking at this remarkable meeting for
some time, and it brings up in my mind, by mere force of contrast, the meeting which I think was most unlike this of any I
have ever attended in London. It was in a small and very shabby
room in the neighborhood of Tottenham Court Road. I do not
suppose there were more than twenty enthusiasts present, but
they were very determined enthusiasts—so much so that they
declined to elect a chairman, because that meant authority, and
they were going to destroy authority. They were a very mild set
of men, and therefore they called themselves Anarchists, as
almost all very mild men do. The difficulty about them was that
they were really not very dangerous men, except one. There was
one man—a young man—there, a pioneer, a fragile and mild
creature, and he really was dangerous, for he had provided himself with a dynamite bomb, on which he was sitting during the
entire time I was addressing that meeting—a fact of which I was
not aware at the time, or perhaps I should not have addressed
them with so much self-possession as I did. Well, taking him as

being the only dangerous man there, who was he dangerous to? Two days afterwards he took his bomb to Greenwich Park and blew himself into fragments with it—unintentionally. That is a thing that many progressive leagues do, though they may not blow themselves to pieces in such a very decisive way. It's almost a pity they don't. You see, not being really dangerous men, and not finding an effective way of quarreling with the world, they very often quarrel with themselves and one another. What interests me about this meeting is that I have some hopes that you are dangerous people. Mr. Campbell has described you as religious people. Well, if you are really religious people, you are really dangerous people, for, after the experience that I have had of various forward movements, I have discovered that the only people who are dangerous are the religious people.

I have been in movements which, as you know, in some ways have been very highly intellectualized. They have been able to give very convincing demonstrations, for instance, to the workingmen of this country that whenever they produce a pound somebody robs them of ten shillings. There was a time about the middle of the last century when many able men—Karl Marx was one—really did believe that if you could only bring that intellectual demonstration and the fact of that robbery home to the working men of Europe they would combine together and rise up against that robbery and put an end to it. I don't know that I hadn't some hopes in that direction myself at that time, when perhaps I was more intellectually active than I have been of late years, but I discovered by experience that no man has the slightest objection to being robbed of ten shillings out of a pound if the remaining ten shillings will make him reasonably comfortable. I find on reflection that although I myself have probably made more money for newspaper proprietors than they always thought it necessary to hand over to me, that fact does not make me uncomfortable, doesn't even put me on bad terms with the proprietors of newspapers. The mere money question does not really move me. I always feel that a certain type of commercial man ought to have a great deal of money— a great deal more money than I have, in fact—because he seems to enjoy that and nothing else, whereas my difficulty in life has been that money is more or less a nuisance to me. I want to get

THE IDEAL OF CITIZENSHIP

a state of communism in which there shall not be any money. I never could understand why people of any business faculty should not be able to average a day's consumption without a pocket full of coppers and having to make all sorts of ridiculous calculations.

However, I don't want to go too far ahead even for this audience. I want to come back to my theme of the hopefulness of the religious character of this league. And, remember, congregations believing themselves to be religious are not a new thing. I want to go back even more than thirty years during which I have been addressing progressive leagues. I want to go back to my own childhood. Also, finding myself in the City Temple, I want to yield to an irresistible temptation to tell a profane story, and it will not only be a very profane story, but it will be a true story, and it will have a certain illustrative value. Now try to imagine me, a very small boy, with my ears very wide open, in what Mr. Gilbert K. Chesterton calls my "narrow, Puritan home." [1] Well, on the occasion which I am going to recall, there were in that narrow, Puritan home three gentlemen who were having what they believed to be a very heated discussion about religion. One was my father, another my maternal uncle, and the third a visitor of ours. The subject of the dispute was the raising of Lazarus. Only one of the parties took what would then, I think, have been called the Christian view. I shall call it the evangelical view, a less compromising term. That view was that the raising of Lazarus occurred exactly as it is described in the Gospels. I shouldn't object to call that the Christian view if it had not involved the opinion, very popular among religious people at that time, that the reason why you admired Jesus and followed Jesus was that he was able to raise people from the dead. Perhaps the reason why some of them always spoke very respectfully of him was a sort of feeling in their mind that a man who could raise people from the dead might possibly on sufficient provocation reverse the operation. However, one of the parties took this view. Another, the visitor, took the absolutely sceptical view; he said that such a thing had never happened— that such stories were told of all great teachers of mankind— that it was more probable that a storyteller was a liar than that a man could be raised from the dead. But the third person, my maternal uncle, took another view; he said that the miracle was what would be called in these days a put-up job, by which he meant that Jesus had made a confederate of Lazarus—had made it worth his while, or had asked him for friendship's sake, to pretend he was dead and at the proper moment to pretend to come to life. Now imagine me as a little child listening to this discussion! I listened with very great interest, and I confess to you that the view which recommended itself most to me was that of my maternal uncle. I think, on reflection, you will admit that that was the natural and healthy side for a growing boy to take, because my maternal uncle's view appealed to the sense of humor, which is a very good thing and a very human thing, whereas the other two views—one appealing to our mere credulity and the other to mere scepticism—really did not appeal to anything at all that had any genuine religious value. I therefore contend that I was right in taking what was at any rate the most amusing point of view. I think you will see that there was a certain promise of salvation in the fact that at that time one of the most popular writers on Bible subjects was Mark Twain, and Mark Twain mostly made fun of them.

But now I want to come to the deeper significance of this scene. The one thing that never occurred to these three men who were urgently disputing was that they were disputing about a thing of no importance whatever. They believed they were disputing about a thing of supreme importance. The evangelical really believed that if he let the miracle of the raising of Lazarus go he was letting Christianity and religion go. The sceptic believed that to disprove the story of the raising of Lazarus was to make a clean sweep of the Bible from one end to the other, and of the whole fabric of religion. Supposing any person had come into that room and said, "Gentlemen, why are you wasting so many words about this? Suppose you take out of the Gospels the story of the raising of Lazarus, what worse are the Gospels, and what worse is Christianity? Supposing even that you add to them another half a dozen raisings from the dead, how much stronger is the position, how much happier is anybody for it?" As a matter of fact, I think such a sensible person would have admitted that my maternal uncle had the best of the situation, as he did squeeze a sort of pitiful laugh out of the controversy, which

THE IDEAL OF CITIZENSHIP

was the most that was to be got out of it. Yet that really was the tone of religious controversy at that time, and it almost always showed us the barrenness on the side of religion very much more than it did on the side of scepticism.

If you come to the sort of religious controversies that are started nowadays—and started very largely by Mr. Campbell—you will find that they are a very much more enlightened kind—that the beliefs from which they start are different. For instance, a man spoke to me lately of the early Christians and of the founder of Christianity. "Well," I said, "I am not exactly an expert on these matters, but you appear to be speaking of Jesus as the founder of Christianity and of the apostles as early Christians. If I am correctly informed by an authority for whom I have very great respect—and he is the preacher at the City Temple—Jesus was not an early Christian. He was a late Christian; his enemies might almost be inclined to sneer at him as a decadent Christian." Now, if you get men thoroughly to realize that Jesus did not come at the beginning of a movement which never did begin except in the sense perhaps that the world itself began somewhere, if you get people suddenly to shift their point of view so decidedly as to see him as the summit and climax of a movement, and then begin to ask why it changed after his death, you then have something worth disputing about. You see men with their minds moved instead of their tempers. You begin to count these men as religious men, and it is the fact that such a change has really taken place that gives me some sort of hope that something may come of your Progressive League.

After all, to come now to the secular part of the matter, you are at a very hopeful moment in the political history of our country. If there were to be a general election tomorrow there would be this astonishing thing about that general election, that for the first time within the recollection of most active men here the election would be about something that we really care for. It is no doubt true that this startling political novelty cannot be attributed to any very deep change of heart on the part of our rulers. I am afraid that it is altogether due to the fact that a few years ago Mr. Chamberlain[2] violently upset a very respectable applecart called Free Trade, and, by suddenly starting a campaign of tariff reform, made his opponents aware that he would keep beating them at the polls unless they found something real to differ from him about at last. And the particular thing they found to differ from him about was the means of raising the revenue. He persuaded the country that it could be raised from the foreigner by tariff reform. It became clear to the party that opposed him that, unless they could raise a good surplus somewhere else, they would be beaten by tariff reform. And accordingly they began to make the sort of speeches that I have been making for the last thirty years. Nobody ever paid much public attention to me, but a great deal of attention is being paid to the cabinet ministers who are now taking a leaf out of my book. You see that it sometimes happens, when men are led by quite interested motives and irreligious motives into religious movements, that they presently begin to get some religion out of the movement. It is quite possible that a cabinet minister who was never in the City Temple in his life, but who on a wet night found himself outside when he had forgotten his umbrella, and the place open, might come in with no other object in life except to get out of the rain. But that would not save him from Mr. Campbell's net, and from going out a very different cabinet minister from what he was when he came in. I have great hopes, therefore, that the numbers of these politicians who are being led by the quite irrelevant circumstances I have described into the progressive arena may possibly find some salvation in your movement.

I must, in conclusion, say that what Mr. Campbell said to you tonight—that your business was to permeate other people —is a very wise saying. I belong to a society called the Fabian Society. In many ways it is a feeble and ridiculous society, but it owes a great deal of the work it has been able to do to not making certain initial mistakes. Other socialist bodies usually proposed to enlist everybody except the capitalists in their own ranks. Their program was: "We will explain our good intentions and our sound economic basis to the whole world; the whole world will then join us at a subscription of a penny a week; then, the whole of society belonging to our society, we shall become society, and we shall proceed to take the government of the country into our hands, and we shall inaugurate the millennium." But what disabled them was that the world wouldn't come in, and while the world remained outside they treated the world more or less as the outsiders, whereas it was really they themselves that were the outsiders. The Fabian Society set its face against that from the beginning. The Fabian Society said that its sound should go out into all lands, but it did not say that everybody else's sound should come into its own little penny trumpet. The Fabian was a man who was never urged to join the Fabian Society. In fact, when he first tried to do it he usually found some difficulty, but, once he was in it, then what he was told to do was to join every other society on the face of the earth he could possibly get into and make his influence felt there. Now, that is what you have got to do.

If you once begin to run your Progressive League in a spirit of hostility to all other leagues whatever, and assume that all the people outside your league are heathens—although you will probably be entirely right in that belief—the assumption will not be a good assumption for you, so you had better not make it. What you have to do is to place before the man who will not take an ideal from you in religious terms—and it is not every-body that can—a simple ideal of citizenship. First you must make it clear that he is not to be a poor man. You must always be down on poor men; you must learn to dislike poverty, be-cause if you don't do that the poor will not listen to you. I tell you, ladies and gentlemen, that the most popular lecture I ever delivered in London was one I delivered at the request of the superior persons at Toynbee Hall who step condescendingly down from the universities to improve the poor. They told me they had a very poor audience—one of the poorest they could get in Whitechapel—and they asked me would I address it, and, when I said yes, they said, "What subject shall we put down?" I said, "Put down this as the subject: 'That the poor are useless, dangerous, and ought to be abolished.'" I had my poor audience, and they were delighted. They cheered me to the echo: that was what they wanted to have said. They did not want to be poor.

What you must say to the ordinary citizen is this: My friend, there are certain things that you ought to do for your country, and there are certain things you ought to demand from your country, and one is as important as the other. You must not submit to poverty either on your own part or anybody else's.

But you must not go about the world thinking or talking of money as if you yourself, by yourself, could make it. It must never come into your mind that any of what is produced in the world has got to belong to you because it could not have been made without your brains and your organizing faculty and your invention and your talent. What every man has to keep before him is this: In the first place his country's claim on him, which is to benefit by his life's work, which he must do for his country to the very best of his ability. You have got in the very short space of life which is yours, and which is your only chance, to give the world everything you possibly can. Remember that there are debts to pay which are debts of honor. There is the debt you owe for your education and your nurture when you were young, and I hope the day will soon come when every person in this country will have a very large debt of that kind. You ought to pay that debt, you ought to pay for the sustenance of yourself in your prime, and you ought to provide for your own old age. And I say that the man who does not feel obliged not only to pay these debts, but to put in something over, so that he dies with his country in his debt, instead of dying in his country's debt, I say that man is not worth talking to.

In return you must demand from your country a handsome, dignified, and sufficient subsistence. Every worker has a right to that, and there must be no question of the nature of the work done. If anything, the men who do the more disagreeable kinds of work should be compensated for their disadvantage.

The duty and the demand I have just put before you have always been the tradition of honorable men in all professions. It is there, waiting to be appealed to. But for a whole century past we have been appealing to the other—the commercial instinct to try and make money for yourself, which has always meant taking away from other people as much as you can. If you will only appeal from that base instinct to the straightforward and honorable instinct, you will find that hundreds of thousands of people round you who have no idea that they are socialists or anything of that kind have that instinct, and that all they want you to do is to show that the thing is possible. Very largely, I think, it will be your business to show that it is possible, but I hope you will also be able to show them that the pursuit of it

　　　　　　　　　　THE IDEAL OF CITIZENSHIP

makes people extremely jolly and extremely happy. Let your pioneers take a leaf out of the book of the Salvation Army. Don't go about with long faces sympathizing with the poor and with ills. Take poverty and illness in extremely bad part, and when you meet a man whose wife is ill or who is poor, and all that sort of thing, don't say to him that it is the will of God, which is a horrible blasphemy. Tell him in solemn Scriptural language that it is a damnable thing and that you have come to try and put a stop to it because you are the will of God. And then you will have put the man you are talking to on the high road to understanding that his will is the will of God too.

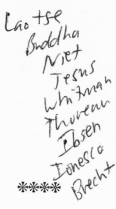

Lao tse
Buddha
Niet
Jesus
Whitman
Thoreau
Ibsen
Ionesco
**** Brecht

Bergson thru Rolling Stones
Iggy & Stooges Werner Herzog
Henry Miller Camus Sartre
SCTV
Bunuel and Altman

THE RELIGION
OF THE FUTURE

Shaw gave this speech before the Heretics Society
at Cambridge on May 29, 1911. The following account is based on the news reports reprinted by
the Heretics in a pamphlet dated July 11, 1911.

[The Victoria Assembly Rooms, Cambridge, were crowded on
Monday evening, when Mr. G. B. Shaw attended a meeting of
the Heretics Society and delivered an address on "The Religion
of the Future." In the audience were to be seen a large number
of the society's most distinguished body of honorary members.
Mr. F. M. Cornford, the chairman, introduced Mr. Bernard
Shaw as a protagonist of the heretical movement, and one who
never scrupled to tell his audience exactly what his opinions
might be on religious questions.

Mr. Shaw began by declaring that his subject was really a
serious one, and that Heretics did not matter with regard to it
—the people who really mattered were orthodox people.]

✸

A Heretic is like a man with a mechanical genius who begins
tinkering with a bicycle or a motor car and makes it something
different from what the manufacturer has made it. Such a man
is a heretic in mechanics; he has a mind and a genius which
enables him to choose for himself. If he has a bad motor car he
makes a good one of it—he makes it to suit himself. The Heretic
is a sort of person who, no matter what religion is supplied at
the shop—by which I mean the nearest church—he will tinker
at it until he makes it what he thinks it should be. The Heretic
is really a man with homemade religion, and if a man can make
a religion for himself at home we need not bother about him—
he will make his religion to suit himself. What we want to

✸29

trouble about is the great mass of people who take religion as they find it—as they get it at the shop. What the Heretics have to do is to prepare a ready-made religion for the next generation for the people who have to accept religion as it comes. It is of the most enormous importance for any community what ready-made article they are supplying in their schools and churches, as a religion, to the community. Therefore, when I am dealing with the religion of the future, remember that I am not dealing with what the Heretics of the next generation will be talking about. They will be discussing and criticizing whatever the religion is, and the great mass of the people will be outside and will have a ready-made religion and will obey laws founded on that religion, many of them founded more or less on the idea that certain courses of conduct are more or less displeasing to whatever force might be moving the world—the main-spring which at present we call God, and might call other names in future—at any rate the driving force.

Now if we want to get any system of this kind we must really get some sort of God whom we can understand. It is no use falling back on the old evasion and saying that God is beyond our comprehension. The man who says he believes in God and does not understand God had much better turn a good, practical atheist at once. Better atheist than agnostic: an agnostic is only an atheist without the courage of his opinions. The actual, practical use we can make of our God is that we can establish laws and morality which we suppose to be the will of God, and if we do not understand God's purpose we cannot do anything of the kind. Therefore we find a large number of people in the country not understanding God who are practically atheists. It is surprising how little we hear of the name of God outside of our places of worship. We hardly ever hear the name of God mentioned in a court of justice, except, perhaps, when a witness is going through the preliminary form of committing perjury, or when the judge has put on the black cap and is sentencing some unhappy wretch to death. In Parliament we never hear about it at all. I do not know whether you ever hear about it in Cambridge, but you will notice that the mention of God has gone completely out of fashion, and that if the name of God is mentioned it is in a perfunctory sort of way, and seems to come as a sort of shock if the person mentioning it does so in the way of taking the current conception of God seriously.

Here in England we have no fundamental religion of our own. Western Europe, of all places in the world, you will say, is, prima facie, the place for the birthplace of a modern religion, yet we have never produced one. We use a sort of Oriental religion as the nucleus of our religion—a lot of legends that we must get rid of. The man who believes the story of the Gadarene swine[1] will believe anything, and we must leave him out as a critical force. Also the man who believes the story of Elisha and the bears[2] will worship anything. But we must not leave such people out of account as a practical fact in the universe, because these are the people for whom we want to found a religion.

Religion virtually went out with the Middle Ages. If we read through Shakespeare's plays we find a man of very great power and imagination, who evidently had no well-considered views of any kind, who produced a mass of plays in which he set forth his own knowledge of humanity in a very wonderful way, and practically left religion out of account. Then we strike the beginning of a commercial age, an age of people who went to church but who gradually began leaving religion more and more out of their lives and practical affairs. There are many people who are made more religious if they have a God who produces frightful calamities. If we study the proceedings of African and, I have no doubt, European kings, we shall find the same thing. In order, however, not to be personal, I shall keep to the African potentates as much as possible. [Laughter] In Africa they had found it generally necessary, when building their palaces, to bury several people alive and to commit a great number of cruel and horrible murders. This was to create an impression on the tribe and show their majesty and greatness.

In Mahometan religion, Mahomet found it necessary to describe the Judgment Day in most revolting and disgusting terms —to introduce intimidation into religion in order to impress the wild and warlike Arabs. The man of genius finds it difficult to make people understand him. I know this, for I am by profession a man of genius. [Laughter and Applause] The difference between a man of genius and the ordinary man is that the man of genius perceives the importance of things. There are a great number of people who do not understand the vital truths of religion, and so the man of genius has to amuse and frighten them with more or less dreadful things.

We have hitherto been governed by a system of idolatry. We made idols of people and resorted to some sort of stage management. Men and women capable of giving orders were taken to the head of affairs—sometimes they took themselves [*Laughter*], and we gave them crowns or gold lace on their collars, or a certain kind of hat, and sat them on a particular kind of chair. Those people generally were a sort of second-hand idol: they said, "I am the agent of the will of another idol. I understand his will and hand it on to you." We generally had to give them such a different income from our own that their way of life would be entirely removed from that of the multitude. They had to wash their faces oftener, live in a different kind of house, and it was out of the question that their sons and daughters should marry the son or daughter of a common man. In democracy we are trying to get human nature up to a point at which idolatry no longer appeals to us. We see that in revolutions, like the French Revolution, democracy went first to the cathedrals and knocked off the heads of the idols of stone. Nothing happened. No crash of thunder stunned the universe, the veil of the temple remained intact. Then the people went to the palaces and cut off the heads of the idols of flesh and blood. Still nothing happened. Cutting off King Charles' head was a sort of vivisection experiment—a much more justifiable experiment than many that take place today, because we learned something from it. But if Cromwell had not died when he did, if he had lived five or even two years longer, he would have been compelled to put the crown on his own head and make himself King Oliver. It was an entire failure trying to make people obey laws in England because they were intelligent laws. The people said they must have a king. And so they took Charles II and made him king. But democracy is progressing. Take myself, for example, a democrat to the teeth. It is no use trying these kings and gods on *me:* I refuse to be imposed on. And, indeed, with my utter lack of the bump of veneration (a phrenologist told me long ago that my bump was a 'ole), I like and respect kings and judges and bishops as men, but they might just as well give up the robes and aprons as far as I am concerned. I do not value their opinions on politics or law or religion any more than if they were plain Mr. Smith.

We are gradually getting more and more rid of our idols, and in the future we shall have to put before the people religions that are practical systems, which on the whole we can perceive work out in practice, instead of resulting in flagrant contradictions as they do at present. People, however, go from one extreme to the other, and when they do so they are apt to throw out the good things with the bad ones, and so they make little progress. The old-fashioned atheist revolted against the idea of an omnipotent being being the God of cancer, epilepsy and war, as well as of the good that happened. They could not believe that a God of love could allow such things. And so they seized with avidity upon the idea of natural selection put forward by Charles Darwin. Darwin was not the originator of the idea of evolution—that was long before his time—but he made us familiar with that particular form of evolution known as natural selection. That idea was seized upon with a feeling of relief— relief that the old idea of God was banished from the world. This feeling of relief was so great that for the time it was overlooked what a horrible void had been created in the universe. Natural selection left us in a world which was very largely full of horrors, apparently accounted for by the fact that it as a whole happened by accident. But if there is no purpose or design in the universe the sooner we all cut our throats the better, for it is not much of a place to live in.

Most of the natural selection men of the nineteenth century were very brilliant, but they were cowards. We want to get back to men with some belief in the purpose of the universe, with determination to identify themselves with it and with the courage that comes from that. As for my own position, I am, and always have been, a mystic. I believe that the universe is being driven by a force that we might call the life-force. I see it as performing the miracle of creation, that it has got into the minds of men as what they call their will. Thus we see people who clearly are carrying out a will not exclusively their own.

To attempt to represent this particular will or power as God—in the former meaning of the word—is now entirely hopeless; nobody can believe that. In the old days the Christian apologists got out of the difficulty of God as the God of cancer and epilepsy, and all the worst powers that were in one, by believing in God and the devil. They said that when a man did wrong he was possessed by the devil, and when he did right that he was possessed by the grace of God. It was, in fact, the conception of "old Nick." It was a conception of enormous value, for the devil was always represented as a person who could do nothing by himself, and that he had to tempt people to do wrong. I implore you to believe that, because it helps you a great deal. People always used to assume that the only way in which the devil could carry out his will was by inspiring or tempting people to do what he wanted them to do. Temptation and inspiration mean the same thing exactly as firmness and obstinacy mean the same thing, only people use the one word when they want to be complimentary and the other when they want to be abusive. Let me therefore ask you to think of God in a somewhat similar nature, as something not possessing hands and brains such as ours, and having therefore to use ours, as having brought us into existence in order to use us, and not being able to work in any other way. If we conceive God as working in that way and having a tremendous struggle with a great, whirling mass of matter, civilization means our molding this mass to our own purposes and will, and in doing that really molding it to the will of God. If we accept that conception we can see the limitations of our God and can even pity him. In this way you can imagine that something—the life-force— through trial and error, beginning in a very blind and feeble way at first, first laboriously achieving motion, making a little bit of slime to move and then going on through the whole story of evolution, building up and up until at last man was reached.

Contrast this position with that of the Christian apologists, and their God, who has to be excused the responsibility of cancer and epilepsy, excused, too, for humanity and the present audience. You require a lot of apology as a visit to the looking glass, coupled with reflections on your life during the past week, would speedily show. The only consolation is that *up to date* God has been able to produce nothing better.

We must believe in the will to good—it is impossible to

regard man as willing his own destruction. But in that striving after good that will is liable to make mistakes and to let loose instead something that is destructive. We may regard the typhoid bacillus as one of the failures of the life-force that we call God, but that same force is trying through our brains to discover some method of destroying that malign influence. If you get that conception, you will be able to give an answer to those people who ask for an explanation of the origin of evil. Evil things are things that are made with the object of their doing good, but turn out wrong, and therefore have to be destroyed. This is the most important conception for the religion of the future, because it gives us what we are at present and gives us courage and self-respect. And it is ours to work for something better, to talk less about the religion of love (love is an improper subject) and more about the religion of life, and of work, to create a world that shall know a happiness that need not be the happiness of drunkenness—a world of which we need not be ashamed. The world must consist of people who are happy and at the same time sober. At the present the happiness of the world is as the happiness of drunken people. I don't mean that everybody who is happy is like the man who is locked up for being drunk, but ordinary men or women, even in the politest society, at present are not happy and do not respect themselves and do not exult in their existence until they have had at least a cup of tea. [*Laughter*] We have all sorts of factitious aids to life. We are trying to fight off the consciousness of ourselves because we do not see the consciousness of a mission, and finally the consciousness of a magnificent destiny.

We are all experiments in the direction of making God. What God is doing is making himself, getting from being a mere powerless will or force. This force has implanted into our minds the ideal of God. We are not very successful attempts at God so far, but I believe that if we can drive into the heads of men the full consciousness of moral responsibility that comes to men with the knowledge that there never will be a God unless we make one—that we are the instruments through which that ideal is trying to make itself a reality—we can work towards that ideal until we get to be supermen, and then super-supermen, and then a world of organisms who have achieved and realized God. We could then dispense with idolatry, intimidation, stimulants, and the nonsense of civilization, and be a really happy body with splendid hopes and a very general conception of the world we live in. In the meantime those of you who have exceptional, expensive educations should make it your business to give such ideals to the great mass of people. If you adopt a religion of this kind, with some future in it, I believe that you can at last get the masses to listen, because experience would never contradict it. You will not have people saying that Christianity will not work out in business; you will get a religion that will work in business, and I believe that instead of its being a lower religion than Christianity, it will be a higher one. Also it will fulfill the condition which I set out at starting: it will be a Western religion, not an Oriental one. Make the best religion you can, and no longer go about in the rags and tatters of the East, and then, when the different races of the earth have worked out their own conceptions of religion, let those religions all meet and criticize each other, and end, perhaps, in only one religion, and an inconceivably better religion than we now have any conception of. [*Applause*]

✳

[Mr. Shaw afterwards answered a number of questions. Among them was one asking his conception of Christ. To this he replied that Christ was one of the attempts, one of the failures. A man who said that Christ was the highest was not worth working with. But though Mr. Shaw considered the figure of Christ as largely mythical and Christianity to a great extent a failure, yet he begged not to be misunderstood; he did not depreciate the great work which Christ helped on, the work of realizing God, or pressing on towards the good, towards the superman.

As regards death, Mr. Shaw disclaimed any desire for immortality, either for himself or for Mrs. Shaw, whose presence, however (he said), called for restrained language on this topic. For its external expression the religion of the future might have the symphonies of Beethoven and the plays of G. B. S. They need not bother about the past. Let the dead past bury the past. The concern of the Heretic was with the future, with the humanity that is to come.

A hearty vote of thanks to Mr. Shaw terminated the meeting, after which it is pleasant to record that the speaker accepted an invitation to become an honorary member of the society. It was a magnificent meeting. Mr. Shaw appeared the very incarnation of G. B. S., gloriously irreverent, transparently sincere, divinely prophetic, and inspiring.]

MODERN RELIGION I

✳✳✳✳   This speech was published as a supplement to the *Christian Commonwealth* of April 3, 1912. It was labeled, "Some Notes of a lecture delivered at the New Reform Club, London, 21st March, 1912." Since Shaw did not ordinarily write out his speeches in advance, he probably relied on a reporter's notes in preparing it for publication. In 1919, he used the same title for another address on the same subject. (See "Modern Religion II.")

First, I wish to justify the importance of the subject. We must have a religion if we are to do anything worth doing. If anything is to be done to get our civilization out of the horrible mess in which it now is, it must be done by men who have got a religion. One of the reasons which have induced me to take up this subject of late years very seriously is the simple observation that people who have no religion are cowards and cads. You may say, "How do you reconcile that with the recent statement of Bishop Gore[1] that, when he wants to get anything done, he finds it is no use going to church people—he has to go to atheists and nonconformists, and people of that kind?" Well, an atheist is not a man who has no religion, any more than a professing Christian is necessarily a person who has a religion. Obviously, the majority of Christians today have not any religion, and they have less of Christianity than of any religion on earth. What I mean by a religious person is one who conceives himself or herself to be the instrument of some purpose in the universe which is a high purpose, and is the native power of evolution—that is, of a continual ascent in organization and power and life, and extension of life. Any person who realizes that there is such a power, and that his business and joy in life is to do its work, and his pride and point of honor to identify himself with it, is religious, and the people who have not got that feeling are clearly irreligious, no matter what denomination they may belong to. We may give this feeling quite different names. One man may use religious terms and say that he is here to do the work of God. Another man, calling himself an atheist, may simply say that he has a sense of honor. But the two things are precisely the same. Any man of honor is a religious man. He holds there are certain things he must not do and certain things he must do, quite irrespective of the effect upon his personal fortunes. Such a man you may call a religious man, or you may call him a gentleman. I almost apologize for using a term which has been so very much discredited. All English men and women are eager to be ladies and gentlemen; yet the things we do to become ladies and gentlemen are just those that steep us in the basest caddishness and the deepest irreligion. That does not alter the fact that if you could get into people an intelligent conception of gentility or gentleness, you might do something with them. If you allow people who are caddish and irreligious to become the governing force, the nation will be destroyed. We are today largely governed by persons without political courage, and that is what is the matter with us.

Have you ever been asked what your religious views were? Under existing circumstances I find it almost impossible to describe myself satisfactorily. Twenty or thirty years ago, when Parliament, in a state of extreme piety, was violently assaulting Charles Bradlaugh for being an atheist and refusing to allow him to contaminate the saintly people at St. Stephens, I took every opportunity of calling myself an atheist publicly. I remember being intensely disgusted with people who held the same opinions as myself and Bradlaugh and persisted in calling themselves agnostics. I said, "You know perfectly well that what is called God by the people who are throwing Bradlaugh downstairs* does not exist, never did, and never will, and even if you are afraid of the term atheist, or dissatisfied because it is only a negative term, nevertheless you ought to stand up and say at least that you are on Bradlaugh's side—that you are very much

---

* In 1881, Bradlaugh was forcibly ejected from Parliament by fourteen ushers and policemen. This was part of Bradlaugh's continuing battle to take the seat to which he had been elected, but from which he had been barred because of his atheism. He was finally seated in 1885.—Ed.

nearer to his beliefs than to the superstitions of his assailants."
Quite a sensation was caused at the first meeting of the Shelley
Society when I said I was an atheist: a couple of pious ladies
immediately resigned—what they supposed Shelley to have been,
I do not know. Later, I found that because I called myself an
atheist, people supposed me to be a materialist. When Bradlaugh died, the National Secular Society, having some temporary
disagreement with his successor, Mr. Foote,[2] wanted another
leader—a thoroughgoing atheist—and accordingly invited various people to address them at the Hall of Science. Among others,
they invited me—no doubt because of my utterances during
Bradlaugh's conflict with Parliament. I chose for my subject
"Progress in Free Thought." As some of them thought their
secularism the final term of the human intellect, they felt that
the man who, having got there, wanted to progress still further,
must be an arch-atheist of all creation. I had an exceedingly
pleasant evening. I do not think it would have been possible
for Bradlaugh to have thrown the most bigoted audience of
Plymouth Brethren into such transports of rage as I did the
freethinkers at the Hall of Science. I dealt with the whole mass
of superstition which they called free thought: I went into their
Darwinism and Haeckelism,[3] and physical science, and the rest
of it, and showed that it did not account even for bare consciousness. I warned them that if any of them fell into the hands of a
moderately intelligent Jesuit—not that I ever met one—he could
turn them inside out. I reminded them that their former leader,
Mrs. Besant,[4] the greatest orator in England, had in an extraordinarily short space of time become a Theosophist, and gone
almost to the other pole of belief. (Curiously enough, Mrs.
Besant had allowed herself to be converted by Madame Blavatsky and Colonel Olcott,[5] but had refused to be converted by me,
although I had been telling her the same things for a long
time.) I then said, "Let us get at simple, scientific facts. Take
the dogmas of the Immaculate Conception, which I firmly believe in, and of the Trinity, which is the most obvious common
sense." Now, in the Hall of Science the Trinity was regarded
simply as an arithmetical absurdity. "Do you mean to say," they
said, "that one person can be three, and three persons can be
one?" I replied, "You are the father of your son and the son of

your father. I am not satisfied with three persons, any more than Shelley was satisfied with three primary colors in the rainbow; he called it the million-colored bow. I am prepared to believe, not only in a trinity, but in a trillion-trinity." "Do you mean to say," they demanded, "that you believe in the Immaculate Conception of Jesus?" "Certainly," I replied, "I believe in the Immaculate Conception of Jesus's mother, and I believe in the Immaculate Conception of your mother." They simply collapsed; they had not the wit to ask me the simple question, did I believe in parthenogenesis? To that question I should have said, "No." But I should have added that parthenogenesis was not the real point of the dogma of the Immaculate Conception. You can imagine how intensely disappointed the National Secularists were with me on that occasion.

Later, when I said in public that my friend, the Rev. R. J. Campbell, had altered my opinion and made me believe that Jesus actually existed, I was described in print by one indignant secularist as having crawled to the feet of Jesus—a very curious way of putting it. Suppose the debate had not been about Jesus, but about Shakespeare, and a gentleman, after making a careful study of Danish history, came forward and showed not only that there had been a prince named Hamlet but that the particular views, the curious doubts, expressed by him in Shakespeare's play had been finding expression in Denmark for about four hundred years before, so that Shakespeare's hero, instead of being the original Hamlet, was practically the last of the Hamlets—just as Mr. Campbell has pointed out that Jesus, instead of being the first Christian was practically the last Christian, for there has hardly ever been one since. And suppose that, in consequence of this gentleman's researches, I had said, "Hitherto I have regarded Hamlet as a fictitious character, attributing to Shakespeare that truth which is proper to fiction and much more important than the truth of the Post Office Directory, but I am now quite prepared to believe there actually was such a person," would any one have accused me of crawling to the feet of Hamlet?

Throughout the nineteenth century scepticism finally concentrated itself in a certain dilemma which is still puzzling people: the impossibility of reconciling the omnipotence of God with his benevolence. James Mill and John Stuart Mill [6] and their circle used to say, "There is no God, but this is a family secret." People then did not shout it out in the way they do today. The slightest sign one now makes of believing in God exposes one to suspicion, almost to the risk of imprisonment: if you preach the Sermon on the Mount to soldiers, you will be promptly clapped into jail. The dilemma is this: An immense number of people in the nineteenth century became atheists or secularists because some person of whom they were very fond died in some agonizing way or contracted some agonizing disease. It was all very well to talk about a God of love, but one could not live in the world without seeing that if he was responsible for everything, he was not only the God of love, but also the God of cancer and epilepsy. It is very easy to get sentimental about a God of love, but not so easy to get sentimental about a God of cancer and epilepsy. Accordingly, you have the position taken up by Shelley, who denounced God as an Almighty Fiend. All strong natures take that line in waking up Moloch worshipers who imagine they are Christians. On the other hand, you had certain attempts to sentimentalize God by ignoring cancer and epilepsy, and talking a lot of charming flap-doodle, and saying love is enough, and love is everything, and God is love. This sickening talk about love, love went on until you got a God who was the sort of sentimental dupe denounced so fiercely by Ibsen's Brand. Brand said two rather striking things. First, he told people they were worshiping a God whom they could cheat, worshiping him because he could be cheated, and because he was sentimental and did not mean business. The second thing he said was, "Your God is an old man; my God is a young one." But even Brand did not mention the absurdity of conceiving God as a person with a sex—the male sex. Nowadays we see that it is ridiculous to keep saying, "Our Father which art in heaven." What about our Mother who art in heaven? The Roman Catholic Church may claim the glory of having seen the need for our Mother who art in heaven, and it is she who has kept it alive. Clearly, if you have a personal God, one of the first difficulties is to determine the sex of that God. The unhesitating way in which people have assumed that there is a personal God and a male God not only shows that they have not seriously tackled the problem, but that, in so far as they have tackled it, they keep up the Oriental idea that women have no souls—though Mahomet did not take that view. At any rate, here is your difficulty: You have your personal God, and he is either an Almighty Fiend, according to Shelley, or a sentimental dupe.

On this point of the dupery, let me emphasize an important aspect of popular religion. In the nineteenth century Karl Marx on the Continent, and Buckle[7] in this country, brought a great mass of evidence to show the immense part that is played in human institutions—in religion, politics, and everything—by the economic foundation of society. Marx may almost be said to have taken the position, "Show me the tools that men work with, and I will tell you what are their religion and politics." That, of course, is an exaggeration; the materialistic basis of history can be overdone. But the curious thing is that neither Marx nor his critics, who are now beginning to abound, have shown how extraordinarily his theory was borne out by the particular forms of religion, of so-called Christianity, that grew up with the spread of the capitalistic system, particularly in the eighteenth century. You have, under the name of Methodism, what is to me quite the most abhorrent and debasing form of religion that exists—the sort of Christianity that centers round the abominable doctrine of the atonement as preached by the followers of Wesley. This doctrine spread tremendously among dishonest small tradesmen. If you want to know precisely the kind of man I mean, you will find him described by one who hated him just as much as I do, a very great man, a great spiritual force. John Bunyan wrote a book called *The Life and Death of Mr. Badman,* and Mr. Badman is the typical small tradesman, and even the typical large tradesman. It is astonishing how much of that book might be republished today as being absolutely contemporary. Bunyan describes among other things a very familiar process gone through today by quite reputable people—the process of becoming rich through successive bankruptcies. Also there is in that book a very striking criticism of the Manchester school [8] and of the principle that was at the base of the old free trader's position—that of buying in the cheapest market and selling in the dearest. Bunyan used those precise terms long before the

Manchester school had come into existence. He said Badman was one of those who would buy in the cheapest market and sell in the dearest, and what is this, said Bunyan, but trading without conscience? It would have saved us a lot of trouble if people would have taken that simple and sufficing statement of the case about the Manchester school. But people would not take it from persons like Bunyan, just as they would not take it from Carlyle, who said, "This free trade is heartbreaking nonsense"—which the Manchester doctrine certainly is.

You will see that when I speak of this capitalistic system, this commercialism, as William Morris[9] called it (people will probably in the course of the next ten years gradually begin to grasp what Morris meant by commercialism), I mean the system of society in which there is no room for a gentleman—that is to say, our present existing state of society. I may describe it very shortly in this way. When we outgrew the medieval system and got rid of the old obligations by which it held the feudal social structure together, all the land and capital got into the hands of one class, and labor into the muscles of another, both of these classes being alike in being abjectly helpless industrially. The man holding the land had no intention of working on it and no knowledge of how to work on it. The laborer did not know how to procure materials and machinery or to keep accounts. The power of direction and organization was lacking to both the propertied and the laboring classes, and both were utterly dependent on them. Now the middle class, originally the only educated class of workers, have the power of direction and organization, or, rather, they have what are called business habits —not quite the same thing. I do not want to flatter the middle class by suggesting that it understands what it does; it mostly understands nothing of the kind. Ninety-nine per cent of our organizing, directing class are people who go into offices and do what was done last time, going through a routine which they do not understand at all. But, still, that routine was originally invented by people who did understand, and it is modified from time to time by people who do understand. At any rate, the people who have got the routine according to our existing system go to a landlord and say, "Hand your land over to us; we will pay you so much every half-year, and you need have no trouble;

you may live quite idly on it." The landlord says, "That is exactly my ideal life; I quite agree." And if no other middle-class gentleman will give more, the bargain is closed. Then these middle-class people go to the capitalist, the man who has more money than he cares to spend, and they say, "Lend us some of your money, and for the use of it we will pay you a dividend every half-year, and you can live idly and not bother about it." The capitalist says, "You are the very man I want to meet." He lends the capital. I need not elaborate the process. The middle-class man then turns to the working classes, and says, "What are you going to do? Have you any land or capital? No. That is because of your drinking and other bad habits. I am a man of capital; I will pay you so much wages; I will be a father to you, if you will work on my land." He organizes industry, builds factories, buys material in the cheapest market, sells his produce in the dearest, pays the agreed-on interest, rent, and wages out of the price and keeps what is left over as his profit.

Now, that, practically, is the system on which our society is founded today. All the old obligations that limited that have been driven away by free trade, by freedom of contract, and so on. All the old restrictions, which represented honor, religion, patriotism, have been got rid of as intolerable restrictions on the liberty of industry, and today you have this capitalist system in full swing. Also, you observe, it makes the middle class practically the brains of society. All the other classes are dependent on the middle class. But we, who are considering society from the religious point of view, must see with misgiving—even with horror —that the phrase that I used a little time ago—that there is absolutely no room in the system for a gentleman—is literally true. The less the middle-class man pays to the workingman, the landlord, and the capitalist, the more he has for himself, and since the other middle-class men help him to grind down the workman while they compete with him in offering rents and dividends to the propertied classes, he flatters and bribes the man of property and sweats and oppresses the working classes. His hand is against every man except the idler. Thus middle-class men get it rooted in their brains that they must make money at other people's expense and be paid for everything they do, that the man who does anything without being paid for it is a fool, and that if any man does more than any other man without being paid extra he also is a fool. That is to say, they all become ingrained and supersaturated cads from one end of society to the other.

To define a gentleman is simple. A gentleman is a man who makes certain claims for himself: for instance, that he shall be able to live a handsome and dignified life, a life that will develop his faculties to the utmost and place him in a respected and honorable position. In return the gentleman is willing to do the utmost for his country that he is capable of and would scorn the idea of a money value being put upon his services. Our system refuses him the position and denies him the opportunity of the service, though it will let him do its political and military dirty work for nothing if he—as it would say—is fool enough.

The religion which emerges from such a system is a reflection of its cheating, its adulteration, its struggle to get as much as possible for as little as possible, and, finally, to get something for nothing. Accordingly there comes from the whole body of commercialized Christians a demand for some means by which God can be cheated into giving free admissions to heaven. The old Christian conception of God was that he was a person who could not be cheated and was very much to be feared. In the Middle Ages they did not bother about the dilemma of omnipotence and benevolence. On the contrary, the old chroniclers would describe a plague or famine, reveling in its horrors, and then, instead of reproaching God, after the manner of the modern sceptic, they would exclaim that these things showed the greatness, the majesty, the power of God, and bow down before him. We are still very largely governed through our admiring contemplation of very wicked things done by persons in high places.

In those days the shopkeeper used to be told pretty roundly that if he put sand in his sugar and cheated the widow and orphan he would go to hell, and he did not like it. But he soon found out a new trick, which was to cheat and oppress and go bankrupt, and then at the end of it bathe himself in the blood of the Lamb and lay his sins at the foot of the cross. This positively gave a zest to evildoing, as the more iniquities people could bring to be washed away the prouder they were. All this was associated with a conception of God as a peculiarly short-tempered and touchy sort of person, who was constantly interfering with the affairs of the world in the most capricious way. I can remember when every atheist was supposed regularly to take his watch out of his pocket and challenge God to strike him dead in five minutes. Over thirty years ago I was in the company of a number of men, some of whom had a scientific education. They were disputing whether Bradlaugh had or had not done this particular thing. I said, "Surely, if it is alleged that God strikes people dead under such circumstances the test is a very practical one." I then took my watch out of my pocket. The whole company instantly rose up in a panic and implored me to stop. I pointed out that my mind had already sent forth the challenge and that if there was anything in the notion I might be expected to perish within the next five minutes. And they were very uncomfortable until the time was up. There you have an illustration of the absurdity and degradation to which religion had been reduced. The whole consciousness of people in the first half of the nineteenth century had got saturated with the idea of continual—I won't say miraculous interferences, because all life is more or less miraculous to every intelligent person—but interferences entirely capricious and anarchic, following no sort of natural law. This was so demoralizing that the ablest people were ready to welcome any sort of theory that would get rid of this kind of God.

You may ask, "What was the difficulty in rejecting the conception straightaway?" The main difficulty was that they could not conceive the world as they saw it, with the wonderful adaptation of organs to their purpose, as being other than a deliberate manufacture, a thing made to a design by some all-powerful designer, until they were shown a way out by Darwin through his theory of natural selection, which destroyed not only the legends of Genesis, but the original religious theory of evolution which prevailed from 1790 to 1830. To that religious theory of evolution we are now returning. What Charles Darwin revealed was the particular method of evolution he called natural selection, by which the apparent adaptation of organs to their functions was shown to be possible without any purpose or design at all, as a result of pure chance. The hole was not made for the cannon ball, the cannon ball made the hole. The intelligent world immediately took Darwin to their breasts, thankful that at last they had got rid of the old interfering deity. Then followed about half a century of absolute godlessness. As Samuel Butler put it, Darwin banished mind from the universe. That suited the commercial system extremely well. The theory of the survival of the fittest made the competitive system positively scientific.

The enthusiasm for getting rid of God was, like all enthusiasms, not very critical. And the reaction against false religion was like all reactions: It emptied the baby out with the bath. Even the naturalist now sees that natural selection is no explanation of many things external to ourselves, still less of many things within ourselves. Our inmost soul may have been a good deal crushed by commercialism, but it has not been altogether killed. I don't think there is a single man or woman, however corrupt and vile, who has not occasionally done things outside his or her individual interests. Thoughtful people see that there must be design and purpose in the universe because they themselves are designers and share a mysterious purpose to make the world better and wiser, whether the change will benefit themselves or not. As far as their individual struggle for existence will allow them, they are trying to further this purpose, and when there is anything in art or religious ceremony that seems to express this, it gives them a curious sort of exaltation and joy. The simple existence of that feeling gets rid of the natural selection hypothesis of the soul. What I want to do is to make people more and more conscious of their souls and of the purpose which has evolved the soul as its special organ.

We have to face the fact that we are a very poor lot. Yet we must be the best that God can as yet do, else he would have done something better. I think there is a good deal in the old pious remarks about our being worms. Modern science shows that life began in a small, feeble, curious, blind sort of way as a speck of protoplasm, that, owing to some sort of will in this, some curious driving power, always making for higher organisms, gradually that little thing, constantly trying and wanting, having the purpose in itself, being itself a product of that purpose, has by mere force of wanting and striving to be something higher,

　　　　RELIGIOUS SPEECHES OF BERNARD SHAW

phys is trap
mental is trap
feeling is it

gradually, curiously, miraculously, continually evolved a series of beings each of which evolved something higher than itself. What you call evil is nothing but imperfection. What Shelley called the malignity of the Almighty Fiend is only the continued activity of the early attempts which, though superseded by later achievements, have not yet been destroyed by them. Cancer is not a diabolical invention to torment mankind; it was once the highest achievement of the organizing force, just as the tiger is not purposely the enemy of man; it is an attempt to improve on the oyster. And this miracle of natural creation is constantly going on. This tremendous power is continually struggling with what we call external nature and is getting hold of external nature and organizing it. Needing eyes and hands and brain for the fulfillment of its purpose, it evolves them. We are its brains and eyes and hands. It is not an omnipotent power that can do things without us; it has created us in order that we might do its work. In fact, that is the way it does its work—through us. When you get this conception of the universe you become religious; you perceive that this thing people have always called God is something in yourself, as Jesus is reported to have said. Read the Gospel of St. John,[10] and you find Jesus always coming back to that point—ye are members one of another—the kingdom of heaven is within you—God is the Son of Man—and at that point they always stoned him; the Pharisees could not stand that. Your purpose in life is simply to help on the purpose of the universe. By higher and higher organization man must become superman, and superman super-superman, and so on.

And what is to be the end of it all? There need be no end. There is no reason why the process should ever stop, since it has proceeded so far. But it must achieve on its infinite way the production of some being, some person if you like, who will be strong and wise, with a mind capable of comprehending the whole universe and with powers capable of executing its entire will—in other words, an omnipotent and benevolent God.

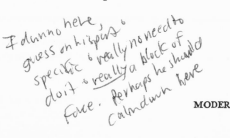

yes- somehow it grows out trying for what?

Life

So physically really may switch to feeling inside evolution of soul therefore blob maybe unimaginable reality of form feeling beyond not higher or whatever just what it is

Life

& it will continue constantly forever so cheer up & relax

he never tries babble about pre "it" just "lives" v on

oh what it rode on the words specifics solv. try to depths estimi nade it why renews it

have you tried to feel it? calm down - feeling of life is all

I dunno here, guess on his part specific really no need to do it really a block of force. Perhaps he should calm down here

WHAT IRISH PROTESTANTS THINK

✲✲✲✲

This speech indicates better than any other Shaw's spontaneous manner and his ability to handle a large audience. He was one of a group of prominent Irishmen called upon to speak on Home Rule by the Irish Protestant Committee. The rally was held at Memorial Hall, Farringdon Street, London, on December 6, 1912. This and a number of the other speeches were published by the Irish Press Agency as a pamphlet with a preface by Stephen Gwynn.

[Mr. George Bernard Shaw proposed the third resolution, which read as follows: "That this meeting expresses its strong desire to see the end of racial and religious feuds in Ireland, and Irishmen of all creeds and classes working together for the common good of their native country."]

✲

I am an Irishman. [*Applause*] My father was an Irishman, and my mother an Irishwoman, and my father and my mother were Protestants, who would have been described by a large section of their fellow countrymen in the ruder age when I was young as sanguinary Protestants. [*Loud Laughter*] Many of the duties of my mother were shared by an Irish nurse, who was a Catholic, and she never put me to bed without sprinkling me with Holy Water. [*Loud Laughter*] Now, why in the name of common decency do you laugh at that? [*Laughter*] What is there to laugh at in an Irish Catholic woman sprinkling with Holy Water—and you know what Holy Water meant to her—a little Protestant infant, whose parents grossly underpaid her? [*Laughter*] The fact that you can laugh at the underpayment of a poor

Irishwoman shows how this open wound of the denial of our national rights is keeping us a hundred years behind the rest of the world on social and industrial questions. I shall make a few jokes for you presently, as you seem to expect them from me, but I beg you not to laugh at them until I come to them. To my mind this relation of mine to my old nurse is not a thing to be laughed at. It is a pathetic and sacred relation, and it disposes completely of the notion that between the Catholic and the Irish Protestant there can be any natural animosity. [*Cheers and Laughter*]

Though I have been before the British public as a political speaker for thirty years, this is the first time I have ever spoken in public on the subject of Home Rule. During that period I have taken part more or less in all the general elections at which Home Rule was at stake. I have heard English party politicians desperately trying to excite themselves about it, and to excite their audiences about it, and I have never once heard them succeed. You may take it from me that the British electorate does not care a rap about Home Rule or Ireland. It is hard enough to induce them to take an interest in their own affairs; it is impossible to make them take an interest in ours. Why should they? [*Laughter*] They know too well that they do not really govern us any more than they govern themselves. Ireland is not governed by Englishmen, but by a handful of Irishmen who exploit our country in the name of England as far as the Irish democracy will stand it.

My own personal feeling in the matter is curiously unreasonable. I do not defend it, but I will tell you what it is. My career has been in many respects a most deserving one. [*Laughter*] I have displayed all the virtues set out in Smiles' *Self-Help*.[1] [*Laughter*] I have won a position of some distinction. [*A Voice: "That was the Holy Water"*] Well, many less plausible explanations are current. [*Laughter*] But the confession I have to make is that, while none of these distinctions which I have achieved by the exercise of the copybook virtues have ever given me a moment's self-complacency, the mere geographical accident of my birth, for which I deserve no credit whatever—this fact that I am an Irishman—has always filled me with a wild and inextinguishable pride. [*Cheers*]

I am also proud of being a Protestant, though Protestantism

is to me a great historic movement of reformation, aspiration, and self-assertion against spiritual tyrannies rather than that organization of false gentility which so often takes its name in vain in Ireland. Already at this meeting pride in Protestantism as something essentially Irish has broken out again and again. I cannot describe what I feel when English Unionists are kind enough to say, "Oh, you are in danger of being persecuted by your Roman Catholic fellow countrymen. England will protect you." [*Laughter*] I would rather be burnt at the stake by Irish Catholics than protected by Englishmen. [*Cheers*] We Protestants know perfectly well that we are quite able to take care of ourselves, thank you. [*Laughter*]

I do not want to banish religion from politics, though I want to abolish the thing miscalled religion in this controversy from the world altogether. I want to bring religion back into politics. There is nothing that revolts me in the present state of things more than the unnatural religious calm in Ireland. [*Laughter*] I do not want a peaceful Ireland in that sense. I want a turbulent Ireland. [*Applause*] All free and healthy nations are full of the turbulence of controversy—political, religious, social —all sorts of controversy. Without it you can have no progress, no life.

Well, in Ireland we Protestant Nationalists dare not utter a controversial word lest we should be misunderstood on the great question of national rights. I have much to say in criticism of Catholicism in Ireland, but I dare not say it lest I should be supposed to be speaking on behalf of Unionism. I have quite as much to say in criticism of Irish Protestantism, but that, too, I must not say lest I should discredit my Protestant colleagues against the day when they will have to claim their share in the self-government of Ireland—and let me say that it will be an important share, for our Catholics are far too amiable and indulgent to take care of public money as Protestants do. [*Applause*]

The Local Government Act of 1898 made a revolutionary change from the most extreme form of oligarchy to the most extreme form of democracy, but we Protestants are kept out of the local councils because it is feared that the return of a Protestant would be a triumph of Unionism. The denial of Home

Rule[2] corrupts every election and every division in Parliament. Consider the Land Purchase Acts.[3] To some of us they are the salvation of Ireland. To me they are its damnation—the beginning of landlordism all over again on a poorer and therefore a worse and more oppressive scale. Many thought as I did, but we all had to be unanimous in support of the acts, because to oppose them would have been to go over to the enemy. We Irish Protestants are bound and gagged at every turn by the Union.

As to the persecution scare, I decline to give any guarantees. I am not going to say, "Please, kind English masters, if you give us Home Rule we will be good boys." We will persecute and be persecuted if we like, as the English do. [*Cheers and Laughter*] We are not children, we do not offer conditions of good behavior as the price of our national rights. No nation should be called upon to make such conditions. Wherever there is a church that church will persecute if it can, but the remedy for that is democracy. We Protestants will take our chance. If you come to that, think of the chances our Catholic priesthood is taking! Look at what has happened to them in free France! Look at what has happened to them in Rome itself! Many of them would be glad enough to be safe in the island of the saints. [*Applause*] I am far more anxious about the future of the unfortunate English when they lose us. [*Laughter*] What will they do without us to think for them? The English are a remarkable race, but they have no common sense. We never lose our common sense. The English people say that if we got Home Rule we should cut each other's throats. Who has a better right to cut them? [*Loud Applause*] They are very glad to get us to cut the throats of their enemies. [*Applause*] Why should we not have the same privilege among ourselves? What will prevent it? The natural resistance of the other Irishmen. [*Loud Applause*]

Mr. Chairman, what I have said must not be taken as a reasoned case for Home Rule as a good bargain for the parties. That is not what we are here for, and it is not what the question will finally turn on. I leave such special pleading to the lawyers who are ashamed to call themselves Irishmen, though they have no objection to be called Irish officials. What I have uttered is a purposely unguarded expression of the real feelings and instincts of a Protestant Irishman. [*Applause*]

CHRISTIANITY AND EQUALITY

❋❋❋❋

Unfortunately the full text of this important address was not reported. It was delivered at the City Temple on October 30, 1913, and the report was printed in the *Commonwealth* of November 5. In the syllabus of the City Temple Literary Society for the years 1913–1914, it was referred to under the title, "Christian Economics."

[The greatest master of challenging ideas in the world—as Rev. R. J. Campbell described Mr. Bernard Shaw—was in his most provocative mood when lecturing on "Christian Economics" at the City Temple Literary and Debating Society last Thursday evening. He had a magnificent audience, better prepared perhaps than any other assembly in England to understand his message. But, even so, he has never spoken with greater effect or with such driving passion. Something like consternation, tempered, perhaps, by the hope that he was not speaking seriously, greeted his opening sentence. But all doubts about his sincerity withered as he proceeded to demonstrate that not merely was the remark true of himself, but of everybody else.]

❋

I must warn you at the outset that, though I am going to lecture on Christian economics, I do not profess to be a Christian. It has always struck me as extremely curious that if you ask the first ordinary Englishman you meet in the street, "Are you a great philosopher?" he will say, "Oh, no!" "Well, are you a poet?" He will give a modest cough because he has written some little things. Ask if he is a capable man of business and he will say, "I do my best." But when you ask him, "Are you a Christian?" he will say, "Of course I am a Christian; how dare you ask me such a question?" I have never professed to be a Christian; that is too large an order for me. I am by profession mainly a dramatist or playwright, and therefore I have no religion whatever in the sectarian sense. In this my position is curiously like that of Jesus himself, who seems to have been regarded by all the sects as a person of no religion.

Christian economics do not really concern us very much until we have begun to make up our minds to introduce Christianity into the world. All our existing civilizations are elaborate organizations for the prevention of Christianity.

Our police and soldiers, all our coercive forces profess to prevent murder and theft, but they do not. They do not profess to prevent Christianity, but they do. The entire social order as we have it at present is anti-Christian.

✻

[Dealing with the question, what is Christianity? Mr. Shaw spoke first of Rev. R. J. Campbell's[1] contribution to our religious consciousness.]

✻

He has restored Jesus, rescued him from the region of fable and legend, and presented him as a credible historical character. The other thing Mr. Campbell has done is perhaps a little more startling; he has made us conscious in the face of the general conviction that Jesus was the first Christian, that he was the last Christian. Christianity was a growing thing which was finally suppressed by the crucifixion.

The crucifixion was a great political success. It seems to have absolutely destroyed Christianity. It was meant to do so by the Jews with the assistance of the Romans. Many people are under the monstrous delusion that Christianity has been flourishing ever since. It is quite true that people after that time called themselves Christians, but as a matter of fact if you go back to the early church you discover that the religion which called itself Christian was in no sense peculiarly Christian at all. It embodied beliefs that were really superstitious. It embodied the idea of the atonement, the idea that you might get rid of your sin by shifting it on to innocent shoulders. That is clearly a doctrine in no way especially characteristic of Christianity. It is

CHRISTIANITY AND EQUALITY

an extremely comforting belief if you have a lot of guilt on your conscience.

It seems to me that we must get rid of that belief in order to make people bear their full share of moral responsibility. I want to destroy the hope in every human soul that we could possibly shift our responsibility for guilt on any sacrifice whatever. Coming to the Middle Ages, there was a religion which also called itself Christian. It was a very fine thing in its way, a very inspiring thing, which produced some of the best works of art in the world. At its best it was a religion of chivalry. But it was tainted with the old notion of sacrifice. It was not Christian. One of the things it never did was to overcome the fear of death. Death is the last enemy to be overcome, and we have not overcome it even yet.

All religions were finally wiped out by modern commercialism, which destroyed every pretence of religion. From the moment that commercialism comes into full swing, anything like a genuine Christian religion vanishes. After that time we have wars, for instance, which are no longer even chivalrous.

✳

[Having thus cleared the field of all rivals, Mr. Shaw proceeded to develop the doctrines he was prepared to call Christian.]

✳

I recognize three main things: We have to give up the idea of revenge and punishment completely and entirely. We have to judge not, that we be not judged. We have to stop putting people into prison who rob and murder; we have to stop scolding and complaining and writing to the *Times*. [*Laughter*] [2] I'm glad you take it in such a light-hearted way. We shall have to take no thought for the morrow what we shall eat and drink; that means we shall have to go in for communism. We have brought the necessity of taking thought for the morrow to such a pitch that very few of us are able to take thought for anything else. And we shall have to adopt the great Christian doctrine which has been recently called the immanence of God.

That is also a rather difficult thing to face, because God is in rather a peculiar position; he is a person who cannot be insured. God has to stand by his mistakes. . . . If we make mistakes we can to some extent get out of the consequences by insurance, but the mistakes of God cannot be insured against; if he makes mistakes—and he evidently makes a good many—those mistakes are absolutely irremediable. And when we adopt this doctrine that God is within us, every mistake we make becomes in magnitude practically like a mistake of God.

✳

[With tremendous force Mr. Shaw made this aspect of his theme a living and terrible responsibility—to make this God within us a sane and very intelligent God.]

✳

If we could imagine what it would mean if the director of the universe went mad, or became wicked, we should begin to understand what is wrong with the world at present. Jesus was always going back to the fact that the son of man was the son of God. He was allowed to preach many other things, but the moment he got on that point the Jews generally stoned him, and they did it because some dim understanding of the meaning of that tremendous doctrine was present to their minds.

✳

[Before passing to deal more fully with his specific subject, Mr. Shaw made the quite startling, and, when one reflects upon it, the profoundly true, observation that if we get rid of revenge and punishment we shall make the position of the evildoer even more terrible than it is now.]

✳

At the present time, when a man is punished for his wrongdoing, we wipe it off the slate. A man can steal, and at the end of three months he is an honest man! Once get rid of the idea of retribution, and evildoers will go about the world absolutely seeking punishment.

By taking no thought for the morrow we are committed to communism. One consequence of the doctrine of the immanence of God will be that we shall realize we are members one of another. There will be no further question of personal and private property. The welfare of one will mean the welfare of all the rest. You cannot have people starving in any Christian country unless everybody is starving. So long as there is food, the food has got to go round. The weak point of communism is that it does not give the consumer any control of production. If all the things that are produced are thrown into the common stock, and everybody comes to take what they want, the result might be that everybody will not find what they want. The only way is to give everybody an equal income. The wonderfully beneficent invention of money makes this possible. When people say that money is the root of all evil they mean either that other people have too much or they themselves have too little. Simple communism is supply without demand—we have no control of supply. True communism will mean that everybody will have an exactly equal income. The income will not be the price of a man. In a Christian state a man being a part of God is infinitely valuable: you cannot buy that little organization in which there is a little bit of God. Equality of income will stop that horrible prostitution of humanity. What we have now is not distribution of income in any sense; it is simple plunder and nothing else.

∗

[Mr. Shaw illustrated the effect of equality of income upon the administration of justice and in politics and then dealt with the physiological argument for his assertion that all incomes should be equal.]

∗

We are a very poor lot of people; we are not good looking. I apologize for being personal, but I must insist that we are not good looking. We are not healthy, we are not strong. But the moment we begin to talk about the better sort of men we have to ask ourselves what sort of man we want to create. There is nothing for us to trust to for the production of a better type of man than the divine spark within us. Love is the only mortal thing we have to trust to in breeding the human race—that curious, instinctive, singular preference, that exception from the rule of general indifference. Nothing is more false than the notion that love is indiscriminating; it is a most fastidious thing. The only hope for improving the human race is by widening the area of sexual selection, so that every young man and maid will be able to go over the length and breadth of the land, and, when they fall in love, will be able to marry—this again points to the need for equality of income.

✳

[The final passages in Mr. Shaw's lecture were a blazing denunciation of the anti-liberal crimes perpetrated by authority in different parts of the world in proof of his assertion that precisely at the time when we are moving forward in matters of social organization, on the moral side of democratic government we are going back.]

✳

A democracy without religion, without the things which I have shown to be the real essence of Christianity, would be a thing so terrible to encounter that one has really to run away from the temptation to be mechanically optimistic. There is no hope for us in economic socialism or in anything else unless we develop our spiritual life. If we do not it will be a very bad thing for this country; it will be a very bad thing for us; it will mean the wreck of another civilization.

✳

[Mr. Campbell's words at the close of the lecture and the nature of the questions put by the audience to Mr. Shaw were a striking evidence of the depths which had been stirred by the passionate earnestness of his final warning.]

MODERN RELIGION II

✳✳✳✳ This lecture was delivered under the auspices of the Hampstead Ethical Institute at Hampstead Conservatoire on Thursday, November 13, 1919, and reprinted in full as a supplement to the *New Commonwealth* of January 2, 1920. The *New Commonwealth* was apparently a short-lived attempt to revive the *Christian Commonwealth*, which disappeared during World War I.

You are the citizens and subjects of an enormous Empire which contains several hundred millions of people. The first thing that any empire or any political organization requires is religion, and it must be a religion which can be accepted by all the persons within that political organization. That may be a simple thing when the political organization is a small one, and consists of people who have all been brought up in the same way, and attended the same place of worship, and had the same teaching, but when it is a political organization which extends over the whole of the earth, which embraces very different climates, very different religions in the sense of organized religions, very different creeds, and so on, then the matter becomes very different.  The official religion of the British Empire would appear to be the religion of the Church of England, an institutional religion, but the difficulty is that the Church of England is supposed to be a Christian religion, and yet in the Empire only eleven per cent of the inhabitants are Christians. Out of every one hundred people in the Empire only eleven are Christians, and a great many of that eleven are a very queer sort of Christian. For instance, a large number of them do not even profess to believe in the Christian religion in the institutional sense, do not attend any place of worship, do not read religious books, do not listen to sermons—some come and listen to me for preference. Is there any likelihood of the principles of the Church of England becoming universally credible? Is there any likelihood of their recommending themselves to the enormous majority who have not yet adopted Christianity and do not show any sign of intending to do so?

Hey don't care

You have the privilege of living at the same time as one of the most distinguished churchmen the Church of England has ever produced. I myself can remember Dean Stanley[1] and Mandell Creighton, the Bishop of London, and they—especially Mandell Creighton—were men of quite extraordinary ability. But at the present time you have a churchman among you who, I think, for intellectual force, for courage and character, for penetration, will probably be remembered quite as long as Mandell Creighton,[2] and I think will possibly take a higher intellectual rank. I mean the Dean of St. Paul's.[3]

Now, the Dean of St. Paul's tells us with reference to those tenets which every postulant for the post of minister or clergyman of the Church of England is required unfeignedly to embrace—that is to say, there are two creeds, there are the Thirty-nine Articles and there is the matter of accepting the Bible as being a perfectly literally true document containing a correct scientific account of the origin of species and the creation—the Dean of St. Paul's tells you that if the bishops were to refuse to ordain any postulant for the clergy who could not unfeignedly and in their plain sense accept that creed, those Thirty-nine Articles and that doctrine about the Scriptures, the clergy would consist exclusively of fools, of liars, and bigots. Those are his words, they are not mine, and this is deliberately told you by the ablest churchman you have, in a position—that of Dean of St. Paul's—which is technically perhaps not quite so high as that of the Archbishop of Canterbury, but really carries with it equal authority, especially when the person who holds it is perhaps rather a cleverer man than the Archbishop of Canterbury.[4] Now, under those circumstances, not only would it appear that there is no chance of whatever genuine religion you are going to make the foundation of your Empire being the Church of England, it would appear to me that if that is true there will very soon be no Church of England at all in the old-fashioned sense of the word. You may anticipate that the church will broaden, that it will relax its tests and so on. You have no historical warrant for believing anything of the kind. Everything you know of the history of these great institutional churches in the past will tend to convince you that as the church is more and more attacked, challenged, instead of liberalizing itself, it will do exactly the other thing, it will draw its lines tighter. It will say, "Sooner than give up our old doctrines we will recruit exclusively from the fools, the liars and the bigots." You know, for instance, that the Roman Catholic Church in the nineteenth century, when it also had to sustain a tremendous attack from modern thought, instead of relaxing its doctrine immediately added to it dogmas which the Middle Ages never dreamed of, and would probably never have tolerated; it drew its lines very much tighter. And when there was a Modernist movement in that church it excommunicated and threw out those Modernists,[5] with an affirmation of doctrine which even the fools, liars and bigots, if I may quote the Dean again, would not venture to impose on the Church of England.

Consequently, I think you must thoroughly make up your minds not merely that whatever the great modern religion is which is going to be a practical religion for the Empire, it will not be the Roman Catholic Church or the Church of England, but it will not be a church at all. You will find that human nature divides itself in a particular way. You meet a kind of man whose religion consists in adhering to a church, who requires a church and requires to be led by a priest, who adopts the creed and articles of a church; he attends the services of the church, and that is his religion. Very often it does not go any further than that, but still, there is the thing for him. To him religion means adhesion to a church and observance of a ritual, and the placing of authority in spiritual matters in the hands of a special class. Now over against the natural-born churchman, there are men of another type, and these men are always really mystics. They do not believe in priests; they very often hate them, and they hate churches. They are deeply religious persons, and instead of priests they have prophets, and these prophets come, if I may say so, practically at the call of God. These men believe in the direct communion of their own spirit with whatever spirit it is that rules the universe. They believe that the inspiration of that spirit may come to anybody, and that he may become a

RELIGIOUS SPEECHES OF BERNARD SHAW

prophet. In the strict sense you may almost say that these people are genuine Protestants; I could say so without any qualification, only unfortunately we have got what many members of the Church of England do not call it, an Anglican Catholic Church. They call it a Protestant Church. If in my native land, you called it a Protestant Church, an Anglo or an Irish Catholic Church, I don't know what would happen to you. The thing would not be tolerated for a moment. I, as a born and baptized Irish Protestant, have always maintained that a Protestant Church is a contradiction in terms, that the genuine Protestant knows no Church and knows no priest. Practically, he believes in the direct communion between himself and the spirit that rules the universe, and the man he follows is a prophet and not an ordained priest, not a man who claims an apostolic succession because a long succession of hands have been laid on heads, and so on; claims practically that apostolic succession is a direct inspiration, which may come to him and which may come to anybody.

Now that distinction between the churchman, between the person the Dean of St. Paul's calls the institutionalist, and the genuine out-and-out Protestant mystic, will always cause a certain division, therefore any religion that is going to unite men will have to be a religion which both of these people can accept. It must have room for mystics, prophets, and for priests, and it must be a religion of such a character as will prevent the priests from stoning the prophets, as they always do. Some of you who have had a perfectly conventional religious education, that is to say an entirely unintelligent one, have been very likely left to draw conclusions for which there is no warrant. For instance, in reading the Bible—you have heard it read in churches, and you have perhaps had it imparted to you by an ordained clergyman —you have derived an impression that the prophets of whom you read were only a sort of old-fashioned clergy. You are entirely wrong in that; they were prophets who were stoned by the old-fashioned clergy. If you read them carefully you will see that they are continually complaining of the persecution which came from the church of their day. You must keep that distinction in mind. And we have to consider this point, as to whether it is possible to get any sort of common ground where you can get a religion for your Empire.

Now, some of you who are thoroughly modern, educated, and intellectual persons may say, "Why do you want a religion for your Empire at all? Why not be pragmatic?" as the modern phrase goes. These religious people are continually pursuing ideals of rightness and truth. "Well," you may say, "in the modern pragmatic way, anything that works is right; anything people believe is true. That is what constitutes truth, and that is what constitutes right." I do not deny that if you wish to be an accomplished man or woman of the world and get on nicely, easily, and sensibly in it you had better be acquainted with this peculiar view. In the ordinary intercourse of society it has its uses. But it is not any use when you come to governing a great state. There it is no use saying that the thing that works is right, because things that you know to be abominably wrong, and that you cannot pretend to be made right by any sort of working, can nevertheless be made to work politically if only you will put sufficient brute force into making them work.

Let me take two particularly atrocious examples of bad and tyrannical government in the modern world. Take, for instance, the government of Russia by the Czars. This I can only describe by saying that if you take as true the very stupidest, the most mendacious, the most outrageous, and prejudiced account that you can find in our more reactionary papers today of the regime of Lenin and Trotsky in Russia, you may assume quite safely that the present state of things in Russia is practically heaven compared to what it was under the Czar, and the fact that we nevertheless made an alliance with that power is a thing that ought to make you very carefully consider whether there may not be some sort of divine retribution in the heavy price we had to pay for making that alliance, and making it with our eyes open.

The other instance of atrociously bad government which has lasted for three or four centuries, I need hardly tell you, is the case of my own country, Ireland. Nevertheless, it worked. The Czar's government worked perfectly, not without a certain amount of friction, because it was made to work by the simple process of getting rid of any person who was opposed to it, putting him in prison, killing him, or otherwise persuading him to be quiet. You will see, therefore, that to suppose a country can

RELIGIOUS SPEECHES OF BERNARD SHAW

be governed pragmatically, that any country can justify its government because it can say it works, is entirely out of the question. Six months of that would knock the pragmatism out of the most inveterate agnostic, the most inveterate shirker of fundamental moral questions you can find anywhere.

In the same way, there is no use in saying that anything the people can be induced to believe to be true is true. That is not so at all, because, just exactly as the most tyrannical state can make a government work, in the same way you will find that that same government, by means of a state church, or by means of an institution like the Holy Inquisition, the Holy Office, as it was called, can also get anything believed. If you kill all the people that don't believe it, or at any rate silence them, get hold of the education of the children, take them from their earliest years and tell them it is true, and it is very wicked to doubt it, you can immediately create such a body of belief as will pragmatically justify the most monstrous creed you can possibly put before the human mind.

Accordingly, when you come to governing a country, then there is no use in talking pragmatism. You have to come back to your old Platonic ideals. You will have to use your reason as best you can, to make up your mind there are certain things that are right and certain things that are true. You may always have at the back of your mind the fact that you may be mistaken, but you cannot sit down and do nothing because you are not sure what you have to do. In governing a country you have to arrive at the best conclusion you can, the conclusion that certain institutions are in harmony with what we call the Platonic ideal of right and truth and trust your instinct more or less to guide you, and also, of course, trust history and experience—except that if you are a politician in this country you will never know anything about history, and your experience is mostly that of trying to cheat other people. Nevertheless, insofar as our laws and creeds can be dictated by persons who have had rather a better preparation for public life than that—gentlemen like the Dean of St. Paul's, although he has certainly had the most frightful antecedents anybody can imagine; no one ever came out with intellectual distinction in the face of such dreadful disadvantages —I must interrupt myself to say that in justice. He is the son of the head of an Oxford college and a doctor of divinity. His mother was the daughter of an archdeacon, and, in spite of that he went deliberately, with his eyes open, and married a lady who was the granddaughter of a bishop and the daughter of an archdeacon. He has been an Eton schoolboy and Eton master. He has taken every possible scholarship that could be got at the University, and how it is he has come out of that with any mind whatever I do not know. It only shows what a splendid mind it is that he was able to stand all that. As I say, if you take men of that type and get them to dictate your creeds and your laws, you will find that they will have to fall back for public purposes on the good old Platonic ideals. They will have to believe in absolute ideas with regard to right and truth, absolute at least for the time. They will have to make an elaborate series of laws in order to maintain what they call right government, and in order to hold up the truth to people.

I rather think that the religion of the future will dictate our laws, particularly our industrial laws—because remember that in the future law will not be the very simple thing it has been in the past, a mere matter of preventing ordinary robbery, I do not mean the robbery from which this country really suffers, which is the robbery of the poor by the rich, but what the policeman recognizes and charges you with as robbery and murder. All that is very simple, but we now know that in the future governments will have to do a great deal more of what they are already doing on a scale which fifty years ago would have seemed perfectly Utopian; that is to say, they will have to interfere in the regulation of industry, will have to dictate the rate of wages, or rather, as a matter of fact, there will not be wages at all. What governments in future will have to recognize as one of their first duties is the very thing they do not interfere with at all, and that is the distribution of the national income among the people of the country. And when you come to that you will see that the religion of the future will be very largely a Marxist religion. That will mean nothing probably to a good many people here because there will be persons who are not socialists and have not read Marx, and persons who are socialists and have only pretended to read Marx but never really have. Therefore I had better explain exactly what I mean. What I mean is that

Anyone can say "Utopia" I dreamit but who can trick people into moving along? That's the rub

one of the things Marx impressed on the world, and he did it to a certain extent by exaggerating it, was that the economic constitution of society was practically at the bottom of everything in society. That was put forward not only by Marx and by Engels, of course, but also by an English historian, Buckle.[6] In his *History of Civilization* you will see the importance he gives to the economic basis, and if one might caricature Marx's position we may suppose him saying something of this kind. Some of the gentlemen in the Natural History Museum at South Kensington will tell you, "If you bring me a single bone of an extinct antediluvian monster, I will reconstruct the entire monster from that bone," which, of course, is an easy thing to do, as nobody can possibly contradict him when he has reconstructed it. Marx may be imagined as saying in the same way, "If you will bring me from any period of history, if you can dig it up, the tool a man worked with, or dig up some evidence of the conditions under which he worked, whether a cottage industry, factory industry, or what not, from that alone I will reconstruct the entire politics, religion and philosophy of that stage of civilization, whatever it was." That, of course, is an exaggeration. Nevertheless, it is enormously important, and it must be recognized in the future by any religious nexus that we may spread, it must be acknowledged that you have to begin with economics. One may illustrate that in a very simple way. Here am I addressing you on a very important subject, a very lofty subject. I am accordingly stretching my intellect as far as I possibly can to rise to the occasion. I have in action all the highest part of me, we will say, all the best bits of my brain for your benefit. Supposing you keep me here for a long time—I know you won't do that, it is extremely likely I would keep you here even when you wanted to go away—nevertheless, supposing you said, "We really cannot stand this fellow with his airs and intellect and philosophy and all this sort of thing, talking about his superiors, like the Dean of St. Paul's and persons of that kind, and daring to criticize. We will take the conceit out of this man; we will see how long his philosophy and lofty ideas, his notions of history, conceptions of the future, will last." You would have nothing to do but to keep me on this platform and take care I did not get anything to eat or drink. You would find that as the hours passed away in spite of all my efforts to keep on a high level, the whole question of religion would gradually fade into the background of my mind, and the question of getting a drink and getting something to eat would steadily grow, and at last you might really bring me to a point at which I would be prepared simply to spring on the chubbiest and nicest-looking persons in this audience and practically eat them in order to save my life. You must remember humanity is like that. The first thing you have got to do if people are to have any religious, intellectual, or artistic life, is to feed them. Until you have done that they cannot begin to have any sort of spiritual or intellectual life. You must attend to that first.

Therefore, I take it the religion of the future, the religion, what ever it is, that is to unite all the races of the Empire and to reconcile them all to one common law, will be, I may put it shortly, a thoroughly Marxist religion, in the sense that it will see that the economic question comes first.

Having said that, I want just to say a word as to how far that religion will be a tolerant religion. There is a great deal of nonsense talked in this country about toleration, and the reason of it is this, that since our national church, the Church of England, began as a heresy—it broke off as you know from the Roman Catholic Church, therefore it began as a heresy—it was persecuted as a heresy, it had to fight under the imputation of being heretical, and the result was it had to fight for toleration, and consequently, it has become a tradition in this country that toleration is an indispensable thing, that you must always tolerate—not that you ever do it as far as you can help it, but nevertheless we have all rather persuaded ourselves that we are tolerant. I do not think any person who has ever candidly examined his own mind would really for one moment suppose he was going to be tolerant. Take, for instance, the question how far do we tolerate the Indian religions? We do tolerate them up to a certain extent; I am not sure we are justified in doing so; but is any person here prepared to tolerate the institution of suttee? The institution by which a woman is encouraged, when her husband dies, to burn herself on his funeral pyre? We have put that down by simple persecution. Indians tell you that if India became entirely self-governing and independent tomorrow, prob-

RELIGIOUS SPEECHES OF BERNARD SHAW

ably there would be a return to suttee by a large class of Indians. The moment you are brought face to face with anything of that kind you perceive you are not tolerant.

In the same way, there are institutions in this country that I am not prepared to tolerate. I am not at all tolerant with regard to children, for instance. In the matter of toleration you have to draw a very distinct line between the religions, the beliefs and creeds which you will allow to be preached to persons who have grown up, who are able to choose and judge, and the religions which you allow to be fed into those children when they are very young and impressionable, when they may have something stamped on them for life which they may never be able to get rid of, and quite unable to resist. If you asked me whether, if I had the power, I would tolerate teaching such a thing to a child as Calvinism, which is the religion of the north of my own country, the good old Ulster of the Calvinists, I would reply that nothing would induce me to tolerate it for a moment, I would not hear of it for one instant. Let the child, if you like, when it grows up to years of discretion even before it ceases to be going to an educational institution—there does come a time when I would say, it is now necessary for the child to learn, as a matter of history and understanding its neighbors, that there is such a horrible belief in the world as Calvinism, such an unspeakable wicked thing, at least as I think, and he must learn also that some people think it an exceedingly nice thing, that the Ulster and a great many Scotch people apparently enjoy it. But as to letting a religion of that kind—or indeed I am not sure that I am in favor of any institutional religion—get access to children when they are very young, I am rather inclined to think children would have to be finally protected against everything but what I have called the modern religion, particulars of which I will come to presently, that is to say the general ideas of right and truth which will govern the politics of the whole Empire; undoubtedly the young children must be governed according to them, but when it comes to tolerating the teaching of religion, I think it is our first duty to protect children against that particular thing, and I should protect them if I had one of these particular creeds myself, and I daresay I have a lot of them sticking to me, I should be quite willing to have children protected

against that just as much as anybody else's. I want you to think
the thing out and remember that although there is a case for
toleration it does not exist in the case of young children, only
in the case of people who are competent to judge, and of course
you must practice the widest toleration, because the probability
is that the most advanced, the most hopeful direction in which
your religion and intellect, your artistic doctrine or philosophy,
is pushing forward and improving itself, is precisely the direction
which will hold you and make you think it is blasphemy, and
for that reason it is very desirable that you should not persecute
movements in that way; you should only persecute in the case
of things which are entirely abhorrent to your nature, and when
you come to do that I am not at all sure you should not do it
thoroughly.

For instance, to go back for a moment to the case of India,
although there is such a tremendous lot to be said for our
method of tolerating religion in India we have had no excuse for
staying in India at all. As long as we are persecuting it, passionately and vigorously saying, "Your Eastern institutions are
abominable, we are going to root them out with fire and sword,"
the probability is we are making India think, we are teaching
India something. It seems to me if the Indians could only come
over here and have a good persecuting go-in at a lot of our
stupidities and idolatries they might improve us a good deal and
in that way there may be something to be said for the domination
of one civilization by another, that is to say the more bigoted and
persecuting it is the more cause there is to suppose it is doing
something, but the moment you get a broad, tolerant, liberal
relation between the two every excuse for your intervention has
gone. As long as you pretend you are in India on a great mission
from God, that you are missionaries, you may have been right
or wrong, at any rate it is a creditable motive. Now that you
tolerate, now that you have said, "Yes, we all have the same God;
it is all perfectly right; we will allow them to practice their religions in that way," where does it lead you? The Indian says, "All
right, what are you here for?" We have to admit we are here
looking after money, because we get money out of you, and we
get berths for our sons in the Indian Service, and so on. All your
excuse is gone and finally under the influence of that you will

have to clear out. That is the advantage of liberal toleration, that it leads to your clearing out, which is exactly what you ought to do, and some of these days will have to do. But remember when the clearing comes about, when you have practically in India what we call a self-determining territory, when you have Egypt and Ireland with practically all their national individual aspirations satisfied, by that time the days of separate nations will have gone, by that time there will have to be bonds; the Empire will probably be a more real thing than it has ever been before. There will still be a Commonwealth, a common interest, bonds of all sorts, therefore there will still remain the necessity for a common religion, a common thing that binds them together in a common ideal of what is right and true.

Now, all this of course is a mere preliminary to my lecture. Some of you thought probably it was just going to be over; you little knew your man. Can we see any convergence towards a common faith, a common belief, on the part of modern men, especially those modern men who have practically discarded the creeds? People who go to church and who are institutionalists by instinct, like to go to a service, who are nevertheless churchmen yet do not believe the literal inspiration of the Scriptures, do not believe the Thirty-nine Articles,[7] find it impossible for instance unreservedly and unfeignedly to believe one article which affirms transubstantiation and the next article which flatly denies it. That is your idea of an English compromise, it is a very British compromise. Nevertheless, there are many people who are sufficiently consecutive in their ideas to find certain difficulties. I suppose none of you has ever read the Articles. I have read them. They are so extremely short that it is very difficult to forget one completely before you go on to the other, and yet you find places in them where unless you can perform that feat it is not easy to see how you can accept the whole thing. But now out of the welter that has ensued on the scrapping of the old creeds, out of this breakup which is indicated by the Dean's statement that practically if you believe what your grandfather and grandmother believed you are either a fool or a bigot or a liar, that is to say if you say you believe them you are a liar and if you do believe them you are either a bigot or a fool—is there anything coming out of this and is there anything coming out of science?

When I was a young man—I was born in the year 1856—when my mind was being formed, as they say, I had very great hopes of science, and the people at that time had extraordinary hopes of science, because science came to us as a deliverer from the old evangelicalism which had become entirely intolerable. There are, of course, people of the old evangelical type about, but I do not think there are any of them here because I am not the sort of preacher they run after. But I can remember when it was quite a general belief that you had a God who was a personal God, of whom they had a perfectly distinct image. He was an elderly gentleman, he had a white beard—I am an elderly gentleman and I have got a white beard, but I am not a bit like him. Nevertheless, there is a gentleman friend of mine, and a socialist, who is exactly like him, and that is my friend Mr. H. M. Hyndman.[8] Those of you who know him will recognize what the God who was believed in in my youth was like. If you have not had the privilege of meeting Mr. Hyndman you had better seek it. If you get Blake's illustrations to Job you will find a picture of the old gentleman there. You may remember how this was focused by the tremendous sensation which was made by Ibsen; the first play with which he practically stormed Europe was the play of Brand's. The one thing one always remembers is that Brand, the hero, meets a young man and they discuss a little theology and Brand says, "Your God is an old man, I have no use for him." That really I think was the first time it suddenly flashed on Europe that after all, supposing God were to be conceived as a young man?

I remember when I was young I had it pushed into me that everything that was pious was old; even when I read the *Pilgrim's Progress,* which I did when a very small child, when I came to the second part even Mr. Valiant-for-Truth I conceived as an old man, at any rate a grownup person. I remember my surprise afterwards when arriving at years of discretion to discover by carefully reading the introduction in verse, which a child always skips, that Bunyan had conceived Valiant-for-Truth as being a young man in all the glory of youth. But in those days the ruler of the universe was an elderly gentleman, and you had to be very careful about that elderly gentleman because the

comedy

one thing he was watching to do at every turn was to strike you
dead. You used to be told if you were not very careful—there
was always one phrase used—if you said anything that implied
the slightest doubt about that old gentleman, you were told
that you would come home on a shutter. I had when young a vi-
sion of the blasphemer, the atheist, the infidel, always being
brought home on a shutter; they were never brought home in an
ambulance, a hearse, or any other way, but always on a shutter.

OK Kids

I can remember, too, when I was a young man I was at a
bachelor party, and they began to dispute about religion. There
was a pious party there and there was a young man who evidently was a bit of a secularist, and they began disputing about
Charles Bradlaugh,[9] who was the great atheist preacher of that
day. It was alleged he had on one occasion in public taken out
his watch and challenged this God, this old elderly gentleman,
if he really existed and if he were the truth to strike him dead
within five minutes. Well, you have no idea of the bitterness of
the controversy. The pious people, of course, alleged it as being
the most frightful and horrible defiance of God that could be
conceived, but the secularist, instead of taking the line you
would expect, passionately denied that Bradlaugh had done anything of the kind. He said Bradlaugh was too good a man. I said,
"Look here; after all, if people do believe this crude thing, that
the world is regulated by a very touchy deity who strikes people
dead, is not that a very practical way of testing it?" And with
that I took my watch out of my pocket. You have no idea of the
effect it produced. Both the secularist party and the pious party
went into transports of terror. Our host had to appeal to me as
his guest, and as a gentleman, not to think of such a thing. Of
course, it being my duty as a guest, I put my watch back and said,
"After all, the thought has come into my head; the challenge may
not have been put into words, but it has been suggested." They
were exceedingly uncomfortable for the next five minutes. You,
ladies and gentlemen, laugh at this, but in those days it was impossible for people to laugh at it; they were too frightened. Even
the sceptical people felt extremely uncomfortable. When that is
what is called religion, then you have got such a horrible op-
pression, the whole thing is such a nightmare, that if anybody

will come and offer any kind of argument by which you can convince yourself you can get rid of it, you will jump at it without being very critical.

The argument that people found it most difficult to get over was the argument from design. You know the old argument: If a savage took up a watch and saw the way it was arranged, even he would say it was not a casual or accidental growth, that it was a thing designed by a designer. Thus in the middle of the century, evolution had been entirely forgotten. Evolution was first introduced about the year 1780, and until 1830 it was very much in men's minds; it was very much discussed. But in 1830 discussion about it had been exhausted, and it was almost forgotten. Then Charles Darwin, a grandson of one of the old evolutionists, Erasmus Darwin, suddenly made a discovery, with Alfred Russel Wallace,[10] not of evolution, but a particular method which simulated evolution, which was called natural selection. You are all probably familiar with Darwinian natural selection, but the point that affects our argument tonight is this, that Darwin was able to show that case after case of what appeared to be the most exquisite adaptation of means to ends, the most perfect evidences of design, apparently unquestionable cases of a thing having been made and designed for a particular purpose, was nothing of the kind, that simply the pressure of environment had produced the appearance. To put it roughly, supposing there was a hole in a wall and somebody found a cannon ball near it which exactly fitted, people used to say that was the very clearest evidence that some intelligent person made that hole in the wall to fit the cannon. Darwin showed it was entirely wrong; the cannon ball knocked the hole in the wall, and nobody meant the hole to be there at all. That is what natural selection means as opposed to the old evolution, and there came, as you know, a fierce controversy between Samuel Butler,[11] whose life some of you have been reading, and Darwin.

People are rather puzzled at the extraordinary ferocity of the quarrel. I have very often told the story, though it is not told in the biography, of Butler saying to me in the courtyard of the British Museum, in a dogged kind of way, "My grandfather quarreled with Darwin's father, I quarreled with Darwin, and my only regret in not having a son is that he cannot quarrel with Darwin's son." Many people reading the biography cannot understand why Butler was so extraordinarily bitter, but the reason was that he was one of the first men to perceive the full significance and meaning of this natural selection of Darwin's which was taken up by the scientific world and then by the whole world and embraced with the most extraordinary enthusiasm as being a new revelation of the beginning of all science and was applied to everything, so that people declared that the whole mass of evolution had been a matter of natural selection. Butler said, "This doctrine banishes mind from the universe. It presents you with a universe which no man with any capacity for real thought dares face for a moment. It takes all design, all conscience, all thought, out of it, and the whole thing becomes a senseless accident and nothing else. My mind refuses to entertain that." And then Butler set himself to work out what genuine evolution was, and although all through his life Butler was very much slighted, and everyone thought Darwin was one of the greatest men of science that ever existed, now we are all coming round to Butler's view.

But why was it people jumped at Darwin in that way? As a rule, people are not fond of science; they are not much given to studying it. The reason simply was that Darwin destroyed the old evangelicalism, the conception of the continually interfering elderly gentleman with the white beard, who was constantly sending people home on a shutter. He took that weight off the human mind, and people were so enormously relieved to get rid of it that they emptied the baby out with the bath. They practically threw aside everything, and they had a curious notion that since the old evangelical views had been taught in connection with morality, they had not only got rid of the mistakes and crudities and superstitions of the old evangelicalism, but they believed they had got rid of religion and right and wrong altogether, and we entered on a period of pragmatism and materialism which has lasted for fifty years, and which has ended in one of the most appalling wars the world has ever seen. You can trace that war exactly to these purely materialistic ideas. We are very fond of blaming the Germans for this; let us not forget it was an Englishman, Darwin, who had banished mind from the universe. We have occasionally said the Germans are only imitators of us, that they steal our inventions and ideas. I am afraid in this case it is right; they did steal scientific materialist ideas and work on them, but in that particular it is not for us to throw stones. England is undoubtedly the place those ideas came from in the first instance.

Such a thing cannot last; it is too entirely against all our poetic instincts. One knows practically as Butler knew that we cannot empty the universe out like that and make the whole thing to be a series of accidents. We know there is intention and purpose in the universe, because there is intention and purpose in us. People have said, "Where is this purpose, this intention?" I say, "It is here; it is in me. I feel it. I directly experience it, and so do you, and you need not try and look as if you didn't." It is like a man saying, "Where is the soul?" I always say to a materialist of that kind, "Can you tell me the difference between a live body and a dead one? Can you find out the life? What has happened? Here is a man struck by a shell; what has happened? He is made of exactly the same chemicals as before, the same silica, the same carbon; you can find no difference whatever. But somehow he ceases to live, and he is going to tumble to bits. What kept him that strange fantastic shape for so many years? What keeps me in this definite shape? Why do I not crumble into my constituent chemicals?" None of these material people can tell me that. It was that continual question. When people began to get frightfully bored by being told everything was sodium and carbon and all that, they said, "We are not interested in sodium and carbon except when we want it on the dinner table; can't you talk of something more interesting?" And the more interesting thing was life, the most intensely interesting thing on earth, and one began to see that right along the whole line of evolution.

You begin with the amoeba; why did it split itself in two? It is not an intelligent thing for anybody to do. You cannot pretend there is any particular accident in that. You cannot see any case that natural selection makes. But somehow the amoeba does it. It finds that perhaps two are better than one, but at any rate it does split itself in two, and from that you have a continual pushing forward to a higher and higher organization. The differentiation of sex, the introduction of backbone, the invention of

confuse "feel" with "will"? anyway

the beyond "purpose" is irrel - term judged by our sit. - rationalize crutch in a way - we don't need to name it - there's more to it all

your life and its "connection"

of course we don't know we can't so can only guess

higher or dif

could be accident - or design

irrel to here 'now "life bside you" no matter what you decide" on y u must transcend it to live here 'now in spont. moment

eyes, the invention of systems of digestion. You have a continual
steady growth, evolution of life, going on. There is some force
you cannot explain, and this particular force is always organizing, organizing, organizing, and among other things it organizes
the physical eye, in order that the mechanism can see the dangers
and avoid them, see its food and go for it, can see the edge of the
cliff and avoid falling over it. And it not only evolves that particular eye, but it evolves what Shakespeare called the mind's
eye as well. You are not only striving in some particular way to
get more and more power, to get organs and limbs with which
you can mold the universe to your liking, you are also continually striving to know, to become more conscious, to see what
it is all driving at.

And there you have the genuine thing, you have some particular force. The Chairman quoted my expression and called
it the "life-force," Bergson,[12] the French philosopher, has called
it the vital impulse, the *élan vital*. You have many names for it,
but at any rate here is a particular thing that is working this
miracle of life, that has produced this evolution and is going on
producing it, and it is by looking back over the long evolution
and seeing that in spite of all vagaries and errant wanderings
one way or another that still the line as it goes up and up seems
to be always driving at more power and more knowledge; you
begin to get a sort of idea; this force is trying to get more power
for itself. In making limbs and organs for us, it is making these
limbs and organs for itself, and it must be always more or less
trying to get more perfect limbs and organs. If it goes on and on
one can perceive that if it is practically given a free hand as it
were, if the obstacles are not too many for it, it will eventually
produce something which to our apprehension would be almost
infinitely powerful and would be infinitely conscious, that is to
say, it would be omnipotent and omniscient. And you get a sort
of idea that God, as it were, is in the making, that here is this
force driving us. You always have the humbling thought when
you are told by your teachers, "God made you," you look in the
looking glass, and say, "Well, why did he make me? Was that
the best he could do?" And when you do not look at yourself
but look at somebody else, the impression is tremendous. You
really do see that somehow or other, assuming that all the or-

ganisms that have been made are visible, are sensible to us, we cannot be satisfied that we are the last word. It really would be too awful to think there is nothing more to come but us. Nevertheless, we may hope if only we give everybody the best possible chance in life, this evolution of life may go on, and after some time, if we begin to worship life, if instead of merely worshiping mammon, in the old scriptural phrase, and wanting to make money, if we begin to try to get a community in which life is given every possible chance, and in which the development of life is the one thing that is everybody's religion, that life is the thing, then cooperation with this power becomes your religion, you begin to feel your hands are hands of God, as it were, that he has no other hands to work with, your mind is the mind of God, that he made your mind in order to work with. Then you not only get an enormous addition in courage, self-respect, dignity, and purpose, get turned aside from all sorts of vile and base things, but you get a religion which may be accepted practically by almost all the churches, as they purge themselves more or less of their superstition. Because, as I pointed out, instead of purging themselves of their superstition, their method is usually to defend themselves against attack by thickening the crust of superstition. In that they kill themselves. But new churches are formed, and in spite of all their efforts even the existing churches become more liberal.

But supposing I talk in terms of this religion which I have haltingly tried to explain to you, what is the great advantage it gives to me personally? It is this. I never have the slightest difficulty in talking to a religious man of any creed whatever; in fact, I get on perfectly well with Roman Catholics and dignitaries of the Church of England if they are really religious. I do not pretend to get on with people who have no religious sense whatever. I should bore them. But if I come across religious people, Indian, or Irish, or Mahometan, or anybody else, we can meet on this common ground. You find that this thing is in everybody, the hope of this thing. The moment you clear up people's minds and make them conscious of this, that moment you discover that the roots of this religion are in every person, and you may get a common bond all over the Empire.

RELIGIOUS SPEECHES OF BERNARD SHAW

This religion you will see growing up all through your literature, not only in Butler and Bergson, and even in my own works, but you find it coming in all directions, distinctly in the novels and poetry of Thomas Hardy, everywhere in Mr. Wells.[13] Mr. Wells goes on at a tremendous rate. You never know what will come. He suddenly rushes out and says, "Hurrah! I have suddenly discovered something no one has discovered before. I have discovered God." He discovers the things that were discovered the first two centuries after Christ. There has also been a tremendous discovery of Christ himself. In the days of the old gentleman with the white beard who sent people home on shutters, Christ himself was almost as great a caricature of what we have on record of the real Christ as the elderly gentleman was of the real spirit of the universe, the life-force. There has been a sort of rediscovery of Christ. People suddenly begin to discover that his religion is a universal religion, and they also begin to discover that there have been other Christs, and that there are Christs even at the present time, that that spirit which was in Christ you will find among Buddhists, among all sorts of persons, persons whom the evangelicals used to call heathen and idolatrous, and used to give large subscriptions to convert them. Then they used to give large subscriptions to convert the Jews. The whole missionary idea of the old evangelicals was entirely wrong, and furthermore, if they had only read their gospels they would have seen it was wrong on the authority of Christ himself. Christ never attempted to establish a church; he was there in the middle of Jews and Pharisees; he never asked any Jew to become a Christian. He did not mean to establish a church. He meant practically he was one of the prophets. What he was dealing with was mysticism. He wanted the Jews to accept something in addition to whatever creed or institution they believed in, to accept his universal religion. He wanted the Gentile also to accept it, the circumcised and the uncircumcised alike, and when he found people wanted to go and act as missionaries, to go somewhere else and try to tear up by the roots some man's religion and substitute their own, Christ told them quite plainly, "Do not do that; if you go and try to pull up what you think are the tares you will pull up the wheat as well." Of course, we never

MODERN RELIGION II

used to listen to that. We sent missionaries. We plucked up as we
thought the tares in their religion, and the result was that the
missionary's convert has become a byword throughout the world
as a person with no religion at all. It turned out that the wheat
had come up with the tares.

destroy lies means push them along
can't hide from them must face them you
do it mostly they will fall or lie will flow
keep push constantly

destroy doesn't mean hide or ignore
it means forget need – no desire to cling or fixate
because relax

when you relax you are truth & no lie can face
you – oppose means new truth or lie falls
all you can do is push self to open & relax

so "destroy" means simply open up   destroy barriers & blocks & fixation
the closed mind in yourself   in yourself – do it by
take a dogma & push it along open it up   using all (rel. phil etc)
& only you can do it inside forget   learn from it & self–
can't hide or run away – accept a new dogma would be that
you can only open & push yourself inside
constantly destroy & create instantaneously

RELIGION
AND SCIENCE

**** This toast to Albert Einstein, to which Einstein replied in German, was made at a dinner at the Savoy Hotel on October 28, 1930, sponsored, in Einstein's honor, by the Joint British Committee of the Societies of Ort-Oze for promoting the economic and physical welfare of Eastern European Jewry. Lord Rothschild presided, and H. G. Wells was among the other speakers.

The next day's *New York Times* and *Manchester Guardian* carried somewhat differing abridgments of the toast and Einstein's reply. A German Gramophone company recorded them and later presented the records to Shaw. There are, however, lapses between records, and at least one short section is completely unintelligible. The speech as here presented is based on all these sources. Both the *Times* and the *Manchester Guardian* of October 29, mention that a "talking film" was made, but it has never been uncovered.

Ladies and Gentlemen: When my friend, Mr. Wells, asked me to take this duty, I could not help wondering whether he realized the honor he was conferring upon me and whether I was able to discharge it adequately. I felt I could only do my best. Here in London we are still a great center. I don't suppose we shall be a great center long—all that will be transferred presently to the United States—but for the moment I am speaking in a capital where the reception of great men is a very common event. We have a string of great statesmen, great financiers, great diplomatists, and great generals—even occasionally an author. We make speeches and we toast them, and we make pictures as we talk. But still the event is not a very striking one. In London things are fixed ahead, and we know where we have to be. In truth, in London great men are six a penny. I know that great men are a very mixed lot, and when we drink their health and make a speech we have to be guilty of scandalous suppression and disgraceful hypocrisy. There is always a great deal to conceal. If you take the typical great man of our historic epoch and suppose that I had arrived here tonight to propose the toast of Napoleon—well, undoubtedly I could say many very flattering things about Napoleon but the one thing which I should not be able to say about him would be perhaps the most important thing and that was that it would perhaps have been better for the human race if he had never been born. Tonight, at least, perhaps it will be for the only time in our lives, we have no suppressions to make, no hypocrisy to be guilty of.

I have said that great men are a mixed lot, but there are orders of great men, there are great men who are great men among small men but there are also great men who are great among great men, and that is the sort of great man whom you have among you here tonight. Napoleon and other great men of his type, they were makers of empires, but there is an order of men who get beyond that. They are not makers of empires, but they are makers of universes, and when they have made those universes, their hands are unstained by the blood of any human being on earth. They are very rare. I go back 2,500 years, and how many of them can I count in that period? I can count them on the fingers of my two hands: Pythagoras, Ptolemy, Aristotle, Copernicus, Kepler, Galileo, Newton, Einstein, and I still have two fingers left vacant.

Since the death of Newton, three hundred years have passed, nine generations of men, and those nine generations of men have not enjoyed the privilege which we are enjoying here tonight of standing face to face with one of those eight great men and looking forward to the privilege of hearing his voice, and another three hundred years may very well pass before another generation will enjoy that privilege. And I must—even among those eight men—I must make a distinction. I have called them makers of universes, but some of them were only repairers of universes. Only three of them made universes. Ptolemy made a universe. Newton made a universe which lasted for three hundred years.

Einstein made a universe which I suppose you want me to say will never stop, but I don't know how long it will last.

These great men, they have been the leaders of one side of a great movement of humanity which has two sides. We call the one side religion, and we call the other science. Now religion is always right. Religion solves every problem and thereby abolishes problem from the universe, because when you have solved the problem, the problem no longer exists. Religion gives us certainty, stability, peace. It gives us absolutes which we so long for. It protects us against that progress which we all dread almost more than anything else. Science is the very opposite of that. Science is always wrong, and science never solves a problem without raising ten more problems.

All these great men, what have they been doing? Ptolemy, as I say, created a universe, Copernicus proved that Ptolemy was wrong, Kepler proved that Copernicus was wrong, Galileo proved that Aristotle was wrong, and now you are expecting me to say that Newton proved that they were all wrong. But you forget, when science reached Newton, science came up against that incalculable, that illogical, that hopelessly inconsequent and extraordinary natural phenomenon, an Englishman. That had never happened to it before. As an Englishman, Newton was able to combine mental power so extraordinary that if I were speaking fifty years ago, as I am old enough to have done, I should have said that his was the greatest mind that any man had ever been endowed with, and he contrived to combine the exercise of that wonderful mind with credulity, with superstition, with delusion, which it would not have imposed on a moderately intelligent rabbit. As an Englishman also, he knew his people, he knew his language, he knew his own soul, and knowing that language, he knew that an honest thing was a square thing, an honest bargain was a square deal, an honest man was a square man, who acted on the square—that is to say the universe that he creates has above everything to be a rectilinear universe. Now see the dilemma in which this placed Newton. He knew his universe, he knew that it consisted of heavenly bodies all in motion, and he also knew that the one thing that you cannot do to any body in motion whatsoever is to make it move in a straight line. You may fire it out of a cannon with the strongest charge that you can put into it, you may have the cannon contrived to have, as they say, the flattest trajectory. In other words, motion will not go in a straight line. If you take a poor man and blindfold that man and say, "I will give you a thousand pounds if you, blindfolded, will walk in a straight line," he will do his best for the sake of the thousand pounds to walk in a straight line, but he will walk in a circle and come back in exactly the same place. Mere fact will never stop an Englishman. Newton invented a straight line. . . . I advisedly say he invented the force which would make the straight line fit the straight lines of his universe—and bend them—and that was the force of gravitation. And when he had invented this force, he had created a universe which was wonderful and consistent in itself and which was thoroughly British. And when applying his wonderful genius, when he had completed the book of that universe, what sort of book was it? It was a book which told you the station of all the heavenly bodies, it showed the rate at which they were traveling, it gave you the exact hour at which they would arrive at such and such a point to make an eclipse or at which they would strike this earth . . .* as Sirius is going to do some day. In other words, it was not a magical marvelous thing like a Bible. It was a matter-of-fact British thing like a Bradshaw.[1]

For three hundred years we believed in that Bradshaw and in the Newtonian universe, as I suppose no system has ever been believed in before. The more educated we were, the more firmly we believed in it. I believed in it. I was brought up to believe in it. Then an amazing thing happened. A young professor got up in the middle of Europe and, without betraying any consciousness of saying anything extraordinary, he addressed himself to our astronomers, and he said, "Excuse me, gentlemen, but if you will principally observe the next eclipse of the sun you will find out what is wrong with the perihelion of Mercury," and all Europe staggered. It said, "Something wrong—something wrong in the Newtonian universe—how can that be?" And we said, "This man is a blasphemer, burn him alive, confute him [?] madman!" But the astronomers only looked rather foolish and they said,

---

* A phrase unintelligible on the recording and not included in the printed versions.—Ed.

"Oh, let us wait for the eclipse," but we said, "No, this is not a question of an eclipse. This man has said there is something wrong with the perihelion of Mercury. Do you mean to say there is something wrong with the perihelion of Mercury?" And then they said, "Oh, yes, we knew it all along." They said, "Newton knew it." "Then why did you not tell us so before?" Our faith began to shake, and we said, "If this young man says when the eclipse comes and gets away with it, then the next thing that he will be doing, he will be questioning the existence of gravitation." And the young professor smiled, and he said, "No, I mean no harm to gravitation, gravitation is a very useful hypothesis, and after all it gives you fairly healthy results, but personally and for my part I can do without it."

And we said, "What do you mean, do without it? What about the apple?" The young professor said, "What happened to that apple is really a very curious and interesting thing. You see, Newton did not know what happened to the apple. The only real authority upon the subject of what happened to the apple was the apple itself! Now apples are very intelligent. If you watch apples carefully you will learn that they behave much more sensibly than men often do, but unfortunately we do not know their language." And the professor said, "What Newton ought to have done would be to see something fall that could tell the story afterwards, could explain itself. He should have reflected that not only apples fall but men fall, and," he said, "I, instead of sitting about in orchards and watching apples fall, what did I do? I frequented cities in quarters where building operations were going on. I knew, as a man of science, that it was statistically certain that sooner or later I should see a man fall off a scaffolding, and I did. I went to that man in hospital, and after condoling him in the usual fashion, saying how sorry I was for his accident and how he was, I came to business. I said, 'When you came off that scaffolding, did the earth attract you?' The man said, 'Certainly not, *gar nicht,* on the contrary the earth repelled me with such violence that here I am in hospital with most of my bones broken!'" And the professor could only say, "Well, my friend, you have been lucky enough to escape without breaking your own back, but you have broken Newton's back." That was very clear, and we turned round and we said,

RELIGION AND SCIENCE

"Well, this is all very well, but what about the straight line, if there is no gravitation, why do not the heavenly bodies travel in a straight line right out of the universe?" The professor said, "Why should they? That is not the way the world is made. The world is not a British rectilinear world. It is a curvilinear world, and the heavenly bodies go in curves because that is the natural way for them to go." And at that word the whole Newtonian universe crumbled up and vanished and was succeeded by the Einsteinian universe.

Now I am very sorry to say it, you know. You must remember that our distinguished visitor could not say that himself. It would not be nice for him to say it. It would not be courteous. But I, standing here in England, I feel that we had better confess it and acknowledge it. Well, I was greatly impressed when I heard these things because I said, "Here is a wonderful man." This man is not merely challenging statements of fact made by scientific men or other men—any man can challenge a statement of fact. The Flat Earth Man lecturing in Hyde Park, he is challenging statements of fact. Our friends at Scotland Yard, not far from here, spend their lives questioning statements of fact. But this man is not challenging the fact of science, he is challenging the axioms of science, and what is more, not only is he challenging the axioms of science, but the axioms of science have surrendered to his challenge. And then came in my special and particular point of view. These are not results worked out by a mathematician, the results of equations marked out on paper, these are the intuitions of an artist, and I as an artist claim kinship with that great authority. I claim to be a man of science, and in the same sense that he is a man of science. I reminded myself that Leonardo da Vinci, the artist, born twenty-one years before Copernicus, wrote down in his notebook—not as the result of elaborate calculation, but as a perfectly simple and plain and obvious matter of fact—he wrote, "The earth is a moon of the sun." And later on the English artist, William Hogarth, a contemporary of Newton—their lives overlapped by thirty years[2] —and when Newton said, "The line of nature is a straight line," William Hogarth said, "The line of nature is a curve." He anticipated our guest. But he was not mathematician enough to work out the entire problem, and so—I flatter myself that I too

RELIGIOUS SPEECHES OF BERNARD SHAW

am an artist—I think my speech will be understood by our guest here tonight.

Now I come to my peroration, I have spoken enough. Within the last month or so there has come to me and come to many of us our visitor's profession of faith, his creed, and that has interested me very much, because I must confess to you that there is not a single creed of an established church on earth at present that I can subscribe to, but to our visitor's creed I can subscribe to every single item. I rejoice as to the new universe to which he has introduced us. I rejoice in the fact that he has destroyed all the old circles, all the old axioms, all the old cut-and-dried conceptions, even of time and space, which were so discouraging because they seemed all so solid that you never could get any further. I want to get further always, I want more and more problems, and our visitor has raised endless and wonderful problems and has begun solving them.

✳

[Here apparently there was some further reference to Einstein's recent "profession of faith, his creed," which Shaw now calls a "confession."—Ed.]

✳

Well, in that confession[3] there is one passage which must touch us all, and that is the eloquent and moving passage in which he has said to us that he has to confess that one of the needs of his nature is a certain solitude.* We may well understand that a man with faculties so much greater than ours must feel lonely among us occasionally. This is a very distinguished assembly, but it is not an assembly composed exclusively of Einsteins, and that he should feel the need for a certain solitude is inevitable. But I have to apologize to him for thrusting all this noisy publicity upon his solitude, but he has come to meet it, and he has come to invite our intrusion for the sake of the poorest of the poor in this world, of whom you have heard something from previous speakers. Well, I will ask him therefore to forgive the

---

* "I am truly a 'lone traveler' and have never belonged to my country, my home, my friends, or even my immediate family, with my whole heart; in the face of all these ties, I have never lost a sense of distance and a need for solitude—feelings which increase with the years." *Ideas and Opinions*, 9. See Note 3.—Ed.

RELIGION AND SCIENCE

intrusion and to remember this: that in our humble little way we all have our little solitudes. My friend, Mr. Wells, has spoken to us sometimes of "the secret places of the heart." [4] There are also the lonely places of the mind. And our minds are so small that instead of, like our visitor, having a spacious solitude in which you can seek the solutions of problems—in which you can contemplate things greater and happier and more wonderful than mankind—we are too often, in our little solitudes, we are like children crying in the dark and wanting to get out of it. Nevertheless, our little solitude gives us something of a key to his solitude. From our little solitude to his great and august solitude, we want to send him our admiration, our good wishes, and our prayers. Now my Lords, Ladies, and Gentlemen, are you ready for the toast? I now give you the toast: Health and length of days to the greatest of our contemporaries, Einstein.

BRADLAUGH

AND TODAY

✳✳✳✳ This speech of Shaw's was one of a series of speeches delivered at the centenary celebration of the birth of Charles Bradlaugh,[1] held at Friends House, Euston Road, London, on September 23, 1933. It is quoted from a memorial pamphlet issued for the Centenary Committee by C. A. Watts & Co., Ltd., and The Pioneer Press.

Mr. Chairman, Ladies and Gentlemen: One of the things that one has to do at this distance of time in speaking of Charles Bradlaugh is to find out what he really stands for in the memories of those who, like myself, personally remember him and in the memories of those who know nothing about his personality and to whom he is only a name. Nothing would be easier than for me to give a long list of his activities in various directions. He was a man of a great many collateral activities. He was not a man of one subject, and yet I want to remind you tonight that he was preeminently a man of one subject. For instance, if I were addressing the sort of polite audience which would expect me to spread myself on every one of the things that might be said about Charles Bradlaugh except the one central thing which they would prefer me to ignore, I might expatiate unctuously on the services he rendered to labor when he got the Truck Acts passed. But we do not think of the Truck Acts in connection with Charles Bradlaugh. When factory legislation is in question, we thing of Lord Shaftesbury.[2] I have no doubt that if Charles Bradlaugh were here tonight he would make Lord Shaftesbury a handsome present of the Truck Acts. To suggest that the names of Shaftesbury and Bradlaugh stand together in our historic imagination would greatly astonish their surviving contemporaries, for Shaftesbury was sustained all through his life by a burning conviction that the official religion of this country was all right, and Bradlaugh was sustained all through his life by an equally burning conviction that the religion of this country was all wrong. And I am here tonight very largely because I also passionately share that conviction. [*Applause*]

Now we are not here tonight to discuss the merits of this or that belief or disbelief. We are here to celebrate the memory of a political genius. Political genius consists in a sense of values, of knowing the relative importance of things. Bradlaugh saw the fundamental importance of the religious question in this country: that was what made him before all things an Anti-Fundamentalist.

Since his death, things have marched his way. A week or so ago a couple of very eloquent sermons were broadcast from London. One of them was by that great man in his way, the Dean of St. Paul's,[3] and the other by that eminent churchman, the Bishop of Chichester.[4] They were both preaching, and preaching with their utmost seriousness, because they were addressing many millions of people. The subject with which they were dealing was the life of Christ, the example of Christ, the possibility of living the Christian life. The sermons were very good sermons, but neither of them contained one single word from which a stranger to our religions and institutions could have gathered that Jesus Christ was anything more than a man. There was not the slightest hint of his being a supernatural event. The Dean of St. Paul's even went a little out of his way to emphasize that the promises made by Jesus Christ at the end of his career, that he would return and establish his kingdom on earth, had not been fulfilled, and that in future we must face the question of Christ's life and example in the light of that fact.

Clearly we have traveled some distance since the death of Charles Bradlaugh; yet few of those who remember him notice that they have changed their opinions. They remember only that it was not considered respectable to agree with him when he was alive, and as they quite forget why—if they ever knew —they still remember Bradlaugh as being a man with whose opinions it was not respectable to agree. They are not conscious of the fact that there has been such a shift of opinion that many church dignitaries have reached a point which I really think would rather have shocked Charles Bradlaugh. He himself shocked people by saying that he was a republican, but if he were here today and were converted to monarchy he would have to apologize for his conversion, for in his time monarchy was the prevalent system of government in Europe. But what is it now? You can with a little trouble still find a king here and there in Europe [*Laughter*], but even the emperors who were mighty in the time of Charles Bradlaugh are on the dole. His republicanism is therefore now beside the point. What really made Charles Bradlaugh the great man that he was was not so much those extraordinary heroic personal qualities which made him an almost superhuman figure for his contemporaries as well as a great platform artist, but that he saw that the religious question was *the* question. It was certainly the question he had most at heart. [*Hear, Hear*] He spoke as a matter of duty about other questions, but on this one he spoke with passion and conviction, facing every peril to himself for the sake of making his opinions known and denouncing and trying to destroy the Bible worshiping superstition they called religion at that time.

It is a curious point that his devotion to this great social service proves that he must have been a deeply religious man, and this is why we could not have chosen a more appropriate place of meeting to celebrate the centenary of Charles Bradlaugh than Friends House. [*Applause*] Our friends the Quakers have got nearer to real religion than any other professedly religious body. [*Hear, Hear*]

His work is not finished. The spadework he did on its foundations was mostly negative work, that is to say that he had to deny. A great deal of it was necessarily denial of falsehoods and exposure of all sorts of irrationalities and superstitions. I wish he were with us today, because he brought us to the point at which we see that negatives are not enough. [*Hear, Hear*] One of the worst of the crimes we are still committing is that we deliberately go on teaching our children lies. [*Applause*] Those of us who are carrying on Bradlaugh's work are like the unfortunate man in the classical inferno, whose punishment it was throughout all eternity to roll an enormous stone up a hill, only to have it crash back on him again every time. That is what is happening to us, and what happened continually to Charles Bradlaugh. He could get at his own audiences and could convert them, but all round him the new generations of children were going into church schools and into all sorts of schools where the Bible was being put into their hands, not as a collection of old literature and fairy tales, as it is, but as a divine revelation. [*Hear, Hear*] If you want to know what it means to get the campaigns of Joshua rubbed into you in your youth as the work of God, you have nothing to do but read the history of the years 1914 to 1918. [*Applause*]

I say, then, that the campaign in which Charles Bradlaugh was a great captain will have to become a positive campaign. [*Hear, Hear*] We shall have to see that in future children shall not only not be told lies but told truths. [*Applause*] Bradlaugh would approve of that because what made him great was that he could not tolerate falsehood. [*Hear, Hear*] That is saying a great deal in a country in which we are all clamoring for falsehood. The moment anybody utters a truth we all rise up passionately and deny it instinctively without thinking. [*Applause*] You can see the effect of that on our statesmen. There are many men who, in their earlier days, are intellectually honest and, like Bradlaugh, have told the truth and fought for the truth, but they end by going into Parliament. They are classed as eminent statesmen when they learn how to give the public what it wants, and that is bunk. [*Applause*] Whatever you got from Charles Bradlaugh you never got bunk. You never got anything that he did not believe. The only thing I regret in his career is that he went into Parliament. It was just the one place that was not fit for him, nor he fit for it.

The British Parliament is the most effective engine for preventing progress of any kind that has ever been devised by the wit of man. We want men who, like Bradlaugh, will risk their liberty for the sake of progress. There are men who shriek out, "Dictator, dictator," if you suggest a revolt against the British parliamentary system. The less liberty they have the more they are afraid of losing it, and when they are dictated to by the boss in all their daily jobs, and by the landlord's rent collector in their homes, and have all their opinions dictated to them by the millionaires' newspapers until they cannot call their souls their own, they thank God that they are free. What these people need to make them capable of real freedom is the right sort of dictator. Bradlaugh would have made a very good dictator of that kind.

I do not, like Lord Snell,[5] owe my conversion to Charles Bradlaugh, because I was ten times as much an atheist as he was before I ever met him, but I do say that he was a great figure, and there he remains, when a great many of his parliamentary contemporaries have completely faded out of our memory and out of history. We have not got any single man of his stamp now. If we had, perhaps we should stop running after the bunk merchants, who have not his sane sense of values. He knew what was wrong. He knew the fundamental rottenness in our education. He felt it, hated it, and fought it. That is the sort of person we need nowadays, for we are so amiable that we put up with anything to make ourselves agreeable. Yet Charles Bradlaugh was not an unamiable man. There are those on this platform who know a great deal more about him personally than I do, and it is they who will testify that he was an affectionate man, and even, like all great orators, a sentimental man. But he hated the wrong thing, and went for it. That, I think, sums up what we admire in Bradlaugh, the sort of thing which makes him an inspiring recollection and makes us wish that we had a few more like him today. [*Applause*]

RELIGION AND WAR

❋❋❋❋ This talk, which Shaw himself never titled, was
broadcast by the B.B.C. to the Empire (by N.B.C.
in the United States) on November 2, 1937. Shaw
was 81 and no longer appeared at public functions.
The speech has had surprisingly wide circulation.
It was published under the title "As I See It" in
The Listener, XVIII (November 10, 1937), and as
"So Long, So Long," in *Vital Speeches of the Day*,
November 15, 1937. It was included in Sarett &
Foster's collection, *Modern Speeches on Basic Is-
sues* (1939). More recently it was reprinted in *The
Shavian*, n.s., I (December, 1953), as "Shaw Speaks
on War," and as "This Danger of War," in Dan H.
Laurence's *Platform and Pulpit* (1961). The Herit-
age recording of it ("Bernard Shaw Speaks") is one
of the best available transcriptions of Shaw's voice
in his later years.

What about this danger of war which is making us all shake in
our shoes at present? I am like yourself. I have an intense objection to having my house demolished by a bomb from an aero-
plane and myself killed in a horribly painful way by mustard
gas. I have visions of streets heaped with mangled corpses in
which children wander crying for their parents and babies gasp
and strangle in the clutches of dead mothers. That is what war
means nowadays. It is what is happening in Spain and in China
whilst I speak to you, and it may happen to us tomorrow.

And the worst of it is that it does not matter two straws to
nature, the mother of us all, how dreadfully we misbehave ourselves in this way or in what hideous agonies we die. Nature can
produce children enough to make good any extremity of slaughter of which we are capable. London may be destroyed, Paris,
Rome, Berlin, Vienna, Constantinople may be laid in smoking
ruins, and the last shrieks of their women and children may
give way to the silence of death. No matter: nature will replace

the dead. She is doing so every day. The new men will replace the old cities and perhaps come to the same miserable end. To nature, the life of an empire is no more than the life of a swarm of bees, and a thousand years are of less account than half an hour to you and me.

Now the moral of that is that we must not depend on any sort of divine providence to put a stop to war. Providence says, "Kill one another, my children, kill one another to your heart's content. There are plenty more where you came from." Consequently, if we want the war to stop, we must all become conscientious objectors.

I dislike war, not only for its dangers and inconveniences, but because of the loss of so many young men, any of whom may be a Newton or an Einstein, a Beethoven, a Michelangelo, a Shakespeare, or even a Shaw. Or he may be, what is of much more immediate importance, a good baker or a good weaver or builder. If you think of a pair of combatants as a heroic British St. Michael bringing the wrath of God upon the German Lucifer, then you may exult in the victory of St. Michael if he kills Lucifer, or burn to avenge him if his dastardly adversary mows him down with a machine gun before he can get to grips with him. In that way, you can get intense emotional experience from a war.

But suppose you think of the two as they probably are, say two good carpenters taken away from their proper work to kill one another. That is how I see it, and the result is that whichever of them is killed, the loss is as great to Europe and to me.

In nineteen hundred and fourteen I was as sorry for the young Germans who lay slain and mutilated in no man's land as for the British lads who lay beside them, so I got no emotional satisfaction out of the war. It was to me a sheer waste of life. I'm not forgetting the gratification that war gives to the instinct of pugnacity and that admiration of courage that are so strong in women.

In the old days, when people lived in forests like gorillas, or in caves like bears, a woman's life and that of her children depended on the courage and killing capacity of her mate. To this day in Abyssinia a Danakil woman will not marry a man until he proves that he has at least four homicides to his credit.

In England, on the outbreak of war, civilized young women rush about handing white feathers to all young men who are not in uniform.[1] This, like other survivals from savagery, is quite natural, but our women must remember that courage and pugnacity are not much use against machine guns and poison gas.

The pacifist movement against war takes as its charter the ancient document called "The Sermon on the Mount," which is almost as often quoted as the speech which Abraham Lincoln is supposed to have delivered on the battlefield of Gettysburg. The sermon is a very moving exhortation, and it gives you one first-rate tip, which is to do good to those who despitefully use you and persecute you. I, who am a much hated man, have been doing that all my life, and I can assure you that there is no better fun; whereas revenge and resentment make life miserable and the avenger hateful.

But such a commandment as "Love one another," as I see it, is a stupid refusal to accept the facts of human nature. Are we lovable animals? Do you love the rate collector? Do you love Mr. Lloyd George, and if you do, do you love Mr. Winston Churchill? Have you an all-embracing affection for Messrs. Mussolini, Hitler, Franco, Atatürk, and the Mikado? I do not love all these gentlemen, and even if I did, how could I offer myself to them as a delightfully lovable person? I find I cannot like myself without so many reservations that I look forward to my death, which cannot now be far off, as a good riddance. If you tell me to be perfect as my Father in Heaven is perfect, I can only say that I wish I could. That will be more polite than telling you to go to the zoo and advise the monkeys to become men and the cockatoos to become birds of paradise.

The lesson we have to learn is that our dislike for a certain person, or even for the whole human race, does not give us any right to injure our fellow creatures, however odious they may be. As I see it, the social rule must be: Live and let live. And as people who break this rule persistently must be liquidated, the pacifists and non-resisters must draw a line accordingly.

When I was a young man in the latter part of the nineteenth century, war did not greatly concern me personally, because I lived on an island far away from the battlefield and because the fighting was done by soldiers who had taken up that trade in preference to any other open to them. Now that aeroplanes bring battle to my housetop, and governments take me from my proper work and force me to be a soldier, whether I like it or not, I can no longer regard war as something that does not concern me personally, though they say that I am too old to be a soldier. And if nations had any sense, they would begin a war by sending their oldest men to the trenches. They would not risk the lives of their young men except in the last extremity.

In nineteen hundred and fourteen it was a dreadful thing to see regiments of lads singing "Tipperary" on their way to the slaughter house. But the spectacle of regiments of octogenarians, hobbling to the front, waving their walking sticks and piping up to the tune of [*Singing*] "We'll never come back no more, boys, we'll never come back no more" *—wouldn't you cheer that enthusiastically? I should. And let me not forget that I should be one of them.

It has become a commonplace to say that another great war will destroy civilization. Well, that will depend on what sort of war it will be. If it is to be like the nineteen hundred and fourteen war, a war of nations, it will certainly not make an end of civilization. It may conceivably knock the British Empire to bits and leave England as primitive as she was when Julius Caesar landed in Kent. Perhaps we should be happier then, for we are still savages at heart and wear our thin uniform of civilization very awkwardly.

But anyhow, there will be two refuges left for civilization. No national attack can seriously hurt the two great federated republics of North America and Soviet Russia. They are too big, the distances are too great. But what could destroy them is civil war—wars like the wars of religion in the seventeenth century. And this is exactly the sort of war that is threatening us today. It has already begun in Spain, where all the big capitalist powers are taking a hand to support General Franco through an Intervention Committee, which they think it more decent

---

*

RELIGION AND WAR

to call a Nonintervention Committee. This is only a skirmish in the class war. The war between the two religions of capitalism and communism, which is at bottom a war between labor and landowning.

We could escape that war by putting our house in order as Russia has done, without any of the fighting and killing and waste and damage that the Russians went through. But we don't seem to want to. I have shown exactly how it can be done and, in fact, how it must be done. But nobody takes any notice. Foolish people in easy circumstances flatter themselves that there is no such thing as the class war in the British Empire, where we are all far too respectable and too well protected by our parliamentary system to have any vulgar unpleasantness of that sort. They deceive themselves. We are up to the neck in the class war.

What is it that is wrong with our present way of doing things? It is not that we cannot produce enough goods. Our machines turn out as much work in an hour as ten thousand hand workers used to. But it is not enough for a country to produce goods. It must distribute them as well. And this is where our system breaks down hopelessly. Everybody ought to be living quite comfortably by working four or five hours a day, with two Sundays in the week. Yet, millions of laborers die in the workhouse or on the dole after sixty years of hard toil so that a few babies may have hundreds of thousands a year before they are born.

As I see it, this is not a thing to be argued about or to take sides about. It is stupid and wicked on the face of it, and it will smash us and our civilization if we do not resolutely reform it. Yet we do nothing but keep up a perpetual ballyhoo about bolshevism, fascism, communism, liberty, dictators, democracy, and all the rest of it.

The very first lesson of the new history dug up for us by Professor Flinders Petrie[2] during my lifetime is that no civilization, however splendid, illustrious, and like our own, can stand up against the social resentment and class conflict which follow a silly misdistribution of wealth, labor, and leisure. And it is the one history lesson that is never taught in our schools, thus confirming the saying of the German philosopher, Hegel:[3] "We learn from history that men never learn anything from history." Think it over.

So long. So long.

NOTES

✳✳✳✳   INTRODUCTION

1. Herman Ausubel, *In Hard Times: Reformers Among the Late Victorians* (New York: Columbia University Press, 1960), 117.

2. Arthur H. Nethercot, *The First Five Lives of Annie Besant* (Chicago: University of Chicago Press, 1960).

3. Bernard Shaw, *Essays in Fabian Socialism* (Standard Edition; London: Constable & Co., 1932), 145.

4. Bernard Shaw, *Platform and Pulpit,* ed. by Dan H. Laurence (New York: Hill & Wang, Inc., 1961), 131.

5. Bernard Shaw, *Sixteen Self Sketches* (Standard Edition; Constable & Co., 1949), 74.

6. The article was written for T. P. O'Connor's *Star* but never published. It was discovered by Dan H. Laurence and printed in the *Flying Dutchman*, Hofstra College's student newspaper, November 23, 1957, p. 3.

7. Letter from Shaw to F. H. Evans, c/o Sidney Webb, August 27, 1895, Berg Collection, A 836 221781B. Shaw had not yet taken the suggestion of his friend Sir Sydney Cockerell to substitute *v* for *w* in derivatives of his name.

8. The essay appeared originally in the *Savoy*. It was published separately by John Luce & Co. (Boston) in 1905 and as *Shavian Tract No. 5* by the Shaw Society (London) in 1957.

9. Quoted in Raymond Mander and Joe Mitchenson, *Theatrical Companion to the Plays of Shaw* (New York: Pitman Publishing Corp., 1955), 43.

10. Shaw, *Sixteen Self Sketches,* 56.

11. Bernard Shaw, *Man and Superman* (Standard Edition; Constable & Co., 1931), xxvii.

12. Richard Albert Wilson, *The Miraculous Birth of Language* (New York: Philosophical Library, Inc., 1948).

13. Bernard Shaw, *Farfetched Fables* (Standard Edition; London: Constable & Co., 1950), 74.

✳✳✳✳   THE RELIGION OF THE BRITISH EMPIRE

1. R. J. Campbell (1876–1956), Congregationalist pastor at the City Temple from 1903 to 1915.

2. John Clifford (1836–1923) and C. Silvester Horne (1865–1914) were active in the Christian Socialist movement. The latter, a Congregationalist minister, was also a Liberal Member of Parliament from Ipswich after 1910.

3. Three Lord Shaftesburys—referring, no doubt, to the Seventh Earl of Shaftesbury, Anthony Ashley Cooper (1801–1885), an independent in politics, but widely known for benevolent social reforms including better working conditions for women and children, a ten-hour factory day, improved tenement housing, and the establishment of "ragged schools" for wayward children.

❋❋❋❋   THE NEW THEOLOGY

1. *The New Theology* was also the title of a highly controversial book by R. J. Campbell published this same year, 1907. (See "The Religion of the British Empire," Note 1, and the introductory note to "The Ideal of Citizenship.") Campbell repudiated much of the book when he returned to the Church of England in 1915 and withdrew it from publication.

2. Charles Bradlaugh (1834–1891), founder and president of the National Secular Society, Member of Parliament from Northampton, and the most vigorous advocate of atheism of his day.

3. See II Kings 2:23–24.

4. Jean Baptiste Pierre Antoine de Monet, Chevalier de Lamarck (1744–1829), a pre-Darwinian evolutionist-philosopher.

5. *On the Origin of Species* was published in 1859.

6. Sir Charles Lyell (1797–1875), British geologist, friend and associate of Darwin.

7. James Ussher, or Usher (1581–1656), Irish Archbishop whose *Annales Veteris et Novi Testamenti* gave a chronology of Scripture that placed the creation in 4004 B.C.

8. Samuel Butler (1835–1902), English essayist, social philosopher, and Utopian satirist (*Erewhon*).

❋❋❋❋   THE IDEAL OF CITIZENSHIP

1. G. K. Chesterton (1874–1936) had recently published his book, *George Bernard Shaw* (London: John Lane, 1909).

2. Joseph Chamberlain (1836–1914), leader of the Liberal Party, later a Liberal Unionist, father of Sir Austin and Neville Chamberlain.

❋❋❋❋   THE RELIGION OF THE FUTURE

1. See Matthew 8:28–33, Mark 5:2–13, and Luke 8:26–33

2. See "The New Theology," Note 3.

❋❋❋❋   MODERN RELIGION I

1. Charles Gore (1853–1932), a leader of the Christian Social Union.

2. G. W. Foote (1850–1915), Bradlaugh's colleague and occasional rival in the secularist movement, succeeded him as president of the National Secular Society.

3. Ernst Heinrich Haeckel (1834–1919), German biologist and philosopher.

4. Annie Besant (1847–1933), writer and orator in the causes of secularism, socialism, and Theosophy. See Arthur Nethercot's study, *The First Five Lives of Annie Besant* (Chicago: University of Chicago Press, 1960).

5. Helena Petrovna Blavatsky (1831–1891) and Henry Steele Olcott (1832–1907), founders with W. Q. Judge of the Theosophical Society in 1875.

6. James Mill (1773–1836) and John Stuart Mill (1806–1873), father and son, Scottish philosophers and economists, "utilitarians."

7. Henry Thomas Buckle (1821–1862), English historian.

8. The Manchester school, supporters of *laissez faire*.

9. William Morris (1834–1896), socialist, artist, and author.

10. The Gospel of St. John—Shaw's Bible scholarship was sometimes faulty. The remark that "we are members one of another" was made by St. Paul to the Ephesians (4:25). The other concepts Shaw here ascribes to John's Gospel do not explicitly appear there. John mentions becoming "children of God" in 1:12, and he does record the threat of Jews to stone Jesus for blasphemy (10:31–39), "Because you, being a man, make yourself God," to which Jesus replies by reminding them of the Eighty-second Psalm, which says, "You are gods." Only Luke (17:20–21) quotes Jesus as saying to the Pharisees, "The kingdom of God is within you." Nevertheless, Shaw's sense that John regarded the kingdom of God as being present (in contrast to the general view of the Synoptic Gospels) is one which finds support among modern scholars, including those of *The Interpreter's Dictionary of the Bible*.

❋❋❋❋   WHAT IRISH PROTESTANTS THINK

1. Samuel Smiles' *Self Help, with illustrations of character and conduct* (London: 1859), popular in a number of revised editions through the 1890's.

2. Irish Home Rule was a controversial issue from 1871 until the establishment of the Free State in 1922.

3. Acts of Parliament in 1885, 1891, 1896, and 1903 provided loans and grants to enable Irish tenants to purchase their own holdings and thus reduce absentee landlordism.

❋❋❋❋   CHRISTIANITY AND EQUALITY

1. See previous notes on R. J. Campbell: "The Religion of the British Empire," Note 1; "The New Theology," Note 1.

2. No one was a more frequent writer of letters to the editor than Shaw himself. A week after delivering this address he became embroiled in an extended debate in the *Times* with the Bishop of Kensington concerning stage morals and censorship. See *The Shaw Review*, III (January, 1960), 1.

❋❋❋❋   MODERN RELIGION II

1. Arthur Penrhyn Stanley (1815–1881), Dean of Westminster.

2. Mandell Creighton (1843–1901), Bishop of London.

3. William Ralph Inge (1860–1954), Dean of St. Paul's from 1911 to 1934.

4. The Archbishop of Canterbury from 1903 to 1928 was Randall Thomas Davidson.

5. The Modernist movement in the Roman Catholic Church began about 1890 and was condemned by Pius X in 1907. The chief victims were Alfred Loisy in Paris and Father George Tyrrell in England.

6. See "Modern Religion I," Note 7.

7. The Thirty-nine Articles form the creedal basis of the Anglican Church.

8. Henry M. Hyndman (1842–1921), socialist leader, founder of the Social Democratic Federation and the National Socialist Party.

9. See "The New Theology," Note 2.

10. Alfred Russel Wallace (1823–1913), English naturalist.

11. See "The New Theology," Note 8.

12. Henri Bergson (1859–1941).

13. Thomas Hardy (1840–1928) and H. G. Wells (1866–1946), English novelists.

✳✳✳✳   RELIGION AND SCIENCE

1. Bradshaw—in England a railway timetable named for a nineteenth-century printer.

2. Their lives overlapped by only twenty-two years. William Hogarth (1697–1764). Sir Isaac Newton (1642–1727).

3. This was probably the article that Einstein wrote for *Forum and Century*, Vol. 84, 193–94, reprinted in *Living Philosophies* (New York: Simon and Schuster, Inc.), 1931, 3–7, and in *Ideas and Opinions*, by Albert Einstein, edited by Carl Seelig (New York: Crown Publishers, Inc., 1954), 8–11.

4. H. G. Wells, *The Secret Places of the Heart* (New York: The Macmillan Co., 1922). A novel.

✳✳✳✳   BRADLAUGH AND TODAY

1. See "The New Theology," Note 2.

2. See "The Religion of the British Empire," Note 3.

3. See "Modern Religion II," Note 3.

4. G. K. A. Bell (1883–1958), Bishop of Chichester, 1929–1958.

5. Lord Henry Snell (1865–1944).

✳✳✳✳   RELIGION AND WAR

1. Before conscription this was apparently calculated to bring social pressure for enlistment.

2. Sir William Matthew Flinders Petrie (1853–1942), English archaeologist and Egyptologist.

3. Georg Wilhelm Friedrich Hegel (1770–1831).

A NOTE ON THE TYPE USED IN THIS BOOK

The text of this book has been set on the Linotype in a type face
called "Baskerville." The face is a facsimile reproduction of types
cast from molds made for John Baskerville (1706-1775) from his
designs. The punches for the revived Linotype Baskerville were
cut under the supervision of the English printer George W. Jones.

John Baskerville's original face was one of the forerunners of the
type style known as "modern face" to printers—a "modern" of
the period A.D. 1800.

✳

The book was composed, printed, and bound
by The Colonial Press Inc., Clinton, Massachusetts.
Typography and binding design by
MARILYN SHOBAKEN